BEYOND WORDS:

The Healing Power of Horses

Bridging the Worlds of Equine Assisted
Therapy and Psychotherapy

ALITA H. BUZEL, PH.D.

authorHOUSE®

AuthorHouse™
1663 Liberty Drive
Bloomington, IN 47403
www.authorhouse.com
Phone: 1 (800) 839-8640

Published by AuthorHouse   05/26/2016

ISBN: 978-1-5246-0030-3 (sc)
ISBN: 978-1-5246-0029-7 (e)

Library of Congress Control Number: 2016905217

Print information available on the last page.

Any people depicted in stock imagery provided by Thinkstock are models,
and such images are being used for illustrative purposes only.
Certain stock imagery © Thinkstock.

This book is printed on acid-free paper.

Contents

PART I
THE BASIS OF EQUINE
PSYCHOTHERAPY FROM A
PSYCHOLOGICAL PERSPECTIVE

PART II
TARGET POPULATIONS AND THE
BUSINESS OF EQUINE THERAPY

PART III

BEYOND WORDS: A PHOTO ESSAY

EXERCISES

Foreword

What is Equine Experiential Psychotherapy (EEP)?

Equine Experiential Psychotherapy is a form of therapy utilizing a team approach composed of a licensed psychotherapist, a credentialed equine specialist, and a therapy horse(s), who work together to elicit growth and healing in their client.

Beyond Words – The Healing Power of Horses describes the various aspects of EEP from a psychotherapeutic perspective, including hands-on exercises embedded in psychological theory, clinical descriptions of client populations, and technical issues dealing with incorporating psychotherapeutic practices in equine-oriented settings.

Why Now?

The world of psychotherapy has grown exponentially in the thirty plus years I have been in practice. In particular, the recognition of the importance of the mind/body connection in emotional healing, the breakthroughs in understanding brain processing, such as the discovery of neuroplasticity, the willingness to go beyond traditional approaches, as in the growing use of EMDR (Eye Movement Desensitization Therapy) for the treatment of trauma, all signify a new willingness to stretch beyond the historical constraints of verbal communication.[1]

---

[1]   EMDR, the reemergence of Eastern meditation techniques such as mindfulness training, and advances in neuroimaging, such as CT and PET scans that allow scientists to discover the power of the brain to rewire dysfunctional emotional responses, all bypass the over reliance on language and neo-cortical processing that have been the hallmark of traditional psychotherapy.

We have come to appreciate that so much of our personal history and soul-forming experiences as children reside in the body's memory, recorded at a time when we had not the words to either understand or record the narrative of our sorrow. It follows that healing from these pre-verbal wounds needs to be addressed via non-verbal interventions.

In addition, the psychic damage resulting from traumatic experiences is embedded not only in our bodies, but is reflected in the hypersensitive, subcortical area of the brain, the limbic system. This primitive area, which is responsible for the basic survival of a species, is triggered by primal emotions such as fear. You see a bear at the entrance to your cave, and you run! Or stand and fight if you are trapped. Limbic responses bypass the mediating effects of words and logical reasoning. By the time you figure out, "Hey, this bear looks hungry" you would be eaten. It follows that healing trauma wounds, such as PTSD, requires non-verbal, powerful corrective experiences.

In instances of both pre-verbal damage and emotional trauma, we have discovered that working with horses has proven to be a particularly effective healing method. Perhaps we should humble ourselves and say "re-discovered," since the power of horses to heal our spirit and soma has been known from time immemorial. We are just catching up to old wisdom!

Who Is This Book For?

Beyond Words has been written for anyone who finds themselves curious about this new breakthrough therapy.

For the Horse Specialists: A growing number of horse people know, from having worked and lived around horses, the power of these animals to connect, heal, and develop trusting and intimate relationships, both within their own herd and with their humans.

Already horses have become wonderful healing partners with people with physical disabilities and emotional developmental issues such as autism, cerebral palsy (CP), and Down's syndrome. Wouldn't it be logical to extend a horse's innate healing ability to people dealing with emotional issues? These possibilities are explored in easy to follow prose with a minimum of psychological jargon.

Let's say you are an equine specialist who has completed your certification and are ready to start your EEP program. Once you begin working with people with emotional issues, you have entered a very complex and confusing world. Even if you are paired with a psychotherapist, who has the responsibility for understanding and treating psychological issues, it behooves you to have some grounding and basic knowledge of therapeutic concepts and terms. It is also the responsibility of the treating facility to ensure that all legal and ethical requirements associated with psychotherapy, are met. If this is sounding a bit intimidating, it should. You take on a great responsibility when you deal with someone who is emotionally fragile. *Beyond Words* can help you navigate this new world.

For the Psychotherapists: If you find yourself drawn to this new animal assisted therapy, congratulations! Reading *Beyond Words* will help you begin to enter the world of horses and learn when and how these intuitive animals can be integrated into your treatment process. The book also covers the team approach utilized in EEP, so each member appreciates the contribution the others make. Having a horse as part of a therapeutic team might be a bit of a challenge, but I invite you to just be curious and open to all possibilities. Learning more about the roles of horses and equine specialists will assist you in determining if this is a form of therapy that might intrigue you.

For the General Reader: If you are reading this Foreward, you already have shown an openness and willingness to explore the power of nonverbal, relationship-based psychotherapy. Perhaps you are looking to try a new form of therapy or are simply curious as to how this equine "thing" works. I have found that simply reading about these innovations can begin to create openings and changes in how we process ourselves and our worlds.

It is my hope that *Beyond Words* can help all readers—equine specialists, psychotherapists, and interested parties alike—develop the kind of teamwork that will bring new, long-lasting healing to our clients. I have met many talented and dedicated horse people during my various EEP experiences and trainings, but I have not found enough highly trained, licensed clinicians to balance the formula. *Nor* have I found enough emphasis being put on the importance of understanding the complexity of dealing with emotionally fragile human souls. The caring dedication I have encountered in the equine specialists has been heart-warming, but does not compensate for the missing wisdom that comes from clinical experience.

My goal in writing *Beyond Words* is to help bridge the worlds of psychotherapists and horse specialists so that each profession has a greater understanding and appreciation of what the other can contribute. And let's not forget the major role of the horse!

Who Am I To Write This?

Let's start with what I am not. Unlike the brilliant people whom I have met during my trainings and along the way, I am definitely *not* a horse expert. You can ask any horse I have ridden or trained with, and they would agree! I am open, curious, respectful, and a fast learner, but I would never pretend to be anything but a perpetual beginner in the horse world.

Up until I turned fifty, my life experiences with horses had been the obligatory trail rides we took in summer camp. When I started riding lessons, as a gift to myself for making it to the half-century mark in one piece, horses seemed like rather big, mindless creatures, fun to ride through forest trails and along beaches, but not much in the way of the warm connection that I had with my various cats and dogs.

A Personal Journey

Then 9/11 happened. The attack was traumatic for all of us living in the City. We were flung from the safety of a beautiful fall morning into a war zone. The roar of fighter planes circling overhead, the acid smell of burning assaulting us, the clouds of smoke rising from the ashes, the images of people trapped in the buildings…all our senses were profoundly assaulted. What was safe and predictable an hour before had transformed into something frighteningly toxic and dangerous.

Almost immediately, my personal pain and fear had to be compartmentalized to enable me to be present for my patients, many of whom were not only traumatized by having survived the blasts but were also grieving for those they lost on that heartbreaking day.[2]

After the attack, my experience of myself and my world shifted dramatically. As Carl Jung would say, serendipity, that charmed angel of fate, created a confluence of events that led me to an exploration of what felt like a mystical realm, the healing power of horses.

I became profoundly aware of how therapeutic it was for me to just spend time in the barn. Around horses, I could relax, breathe, and feel safe and centered. I was freed from having to talk or listen or cut off my own pain to care for others. Here, in the stable, I could quietly come back to myself simply by being around these gentle giants who asked nothing of me. Being in the barn, being around horses, became my therapy. Just grooming my horse, or leaning on him and letting him bear my weight, was all I seemed to need.

A few years later, I fell off my horse, breaking my arm and putting me out of commission for over six months. A very dear, intuitive friend bought me *The Tao Of Equus* (Linda Kohanov) as a get-well gift. Again, the timing was fortuitous. I knew,

---

[2]   As a therapeutic consultant with the New York City Police Department, I worked with many clients who were first responders on 9/11.

first hand, the healing power of horses from my experience after 9/11, and here was someone who had transformed this wisdom into a potent form of psychotherapy.

I was intrigued by the possibility of integrating horses into my practice. The inherent compassion and wisdom of horses, their ability to balance their wiring as prey animals with their instinctual desire to just relax and graze, their instinct to take care of their own and their loyalty to the herd not only intrigued me, but charmed me. They were also playful and curious, things that rang true to the little girl in me!

Curiosity and Experimentation and Clinical Expertise

Thus my interest in Equine Experiential Therapy developed from my personal, transformational experiences with horses wedded with my training and background as a psychologist. And my perpetual "I wonder what would happen if…" curiosity.

Sitting in sessions with my patients, I often found myself thinking about how great it would be to have them work with horses. As just one example, I was working with a lovely young woman who simple could not say "no" to any request made of her. She thought it would be disastrous to deny someone something; they would hate her, they would think she wasn't a nice person, there would be a big flare up and ugly confrontation. What would it be like if she learned to hold her ground with a big horse? She came out to the barn and through her interaction with the horses found that she did, after all, have the inner power to say "no." And the horse didn't hate her and there were no frightening confrontations. In fact, the horse really took to her and spent the rest of the day by her side. I was impressed with how she brought this empowering experience back into her life.

The more I was able to work with my patients with horses, in groups and one on one, the more impressed I became by the inherent potential of this form of therapy. Along with this interest and curiosity, what I *could* bring to the field of EEP was thirty-years of academic and clinical expertise as a psychologist, including the following:

Specialized Training:

- Pre and post-doctoral training in neuropsychology.
- Clinical Internship at the Brooklyn Veterans Administration Hospital working with soldiers returning from the Viet Nam War who were diagnosed with PTSD, alcoholism, and/or drug abuse.
- Clinical training in rehabilitation psychology at both Bellevue and Rusk Institute.
- Certification in Cognitive Behavioral Therapy (CBT).
- EMDR (Eye Movement Desensitization and Reprocessing) Level I & II.
- Training in early and long-term interventions for trauma-related issues (incest, rape, spousal abuse).

Clinical Work History:

- Consulting and referral psychologist for the New York City Police Department in their Alcoholism Employee Assistance Program (EAP) and their Early Intervention Unit, the division assigned to debrief police after any disturbing incident, e.g. having shot someone.
- Head neuropsychologist in a day-treatment program for young adults with acquired brain injuries (based on the Israeli model of brain rehabilitation) at the International Center For The Disabled (ICD).
- Staff member of The Cognitive Therapy Center of New York.
- Private practice including work with individuals, couples, family and groups.

I hold a Ph.D. in Clinical Psychology and a Masters in both Psychology and Sociology.

Despite all the stuffy credentialing stuff, I am quite a playful person and am more than willing to try new things, fail miserably, laugh, and keep going! Ask any of my horse riding buddies, or for that matter, the horses I have had the pleasure to train with.

EEP Credentials

Being dutifully trained as an academic, I began to research the different schools of thought and training opportunities for EEP. I started by reading everything I could find on the topic of equine experiential psychotherapy.

After my short, intensive home-study program, the next step was to actually try my hand at equine psychotherapy and find out how it felt. I had the theories, I wanted the experience. It was my luck and good fortune that I found Barbara Rector's Adventures In Awareness (AIA) program in Tucson, Arizona. Barbara has been credited with the development of Equine Facilitated Psychotherapy. My three-day, one-on-one intensive with her was one of the most powerful, spiritually enhancing experiences of my life. The effort to stay aware, stay mindful, and stay connected felt like an Olympic psychic challenge. And it was so much fun! I came away from the training convinced that I was on the path I was meant to be on.

Additionally, my equine experiential psychotherapy practical experience has included:

- A week-long, one-on-one riding workshop in Mexico with a horse specialist in 2010 as therapy to get over my then newly developed fear of riding;[3]
- Volunteering at two riding centers for the disabled; one in Manhattan, the other on Long Island.
- A three-day Adventures in Awareness (AIA) intensive with Barbara Rector.
- EAGALA certification (International Association for Equine Assisted Psychotherapy and Learning), Summer, 2016.[4]

---

[3] I had taken a bad fall off my horse, resulting in a broken arm and a couple of operations. It took me all my courage to get back on a horse. Mexico did its magic and by the end of the week, I was galloping across newly harvested farmland and meandering through rock-strewn streams.

[4] The EPE field is generating a number of certifications and training programs offering different models and styles of Equine Experiential Psychotherapy. I highly recommend finding a program that requires its mental health practitioners to be licensed psychotherapists. A more in-depth discussion of the various programs can be found in Appendix I.

- Workshops with my patients, both in groups and as individuals, with the aid of my trusty horse specialist, Rebecca Robin Wilson at Robin's Nest, her charming stable in Sagaponak, New York.

After my training, I was eager to get in the EEP saddle. I had a wonderful equine specialist, Rebecca Wilson, who is a Certified Advanced Riding Instructor (AI Instructor) from the British Horse Society (BHS), to assist me as I stumbled through my first EEP sessions. It helped that Becky's barn was a warm and inviting place and that I had my choice of very lovely, people-friendly, calm horses, particularly Sonny and Mitt, who would do anything Becky asked of them. It also helped that my first "guinea pig" patient group had been working with me as a therapist for years, and they were as curious and open as the horses were.

What I learned about them in that first workshop awed me. I thought I intimately knew these women, yet I was humbled by how much insight I gained by simply watching them interact with a horse. And, yes, they came away from the experience with many insights and feelings that were new and useful for them. Working with the horses has now become an annual event that we all enjoy.

In sum, I beg my readers' patience and indulgence if I stumble in my equine knowledge…just pick me up and put me back on my horse. I am happy to bring the psychotherapeutic expertise I have to share with my team!

Looking Forward

What has struck me as I have worked with Equine Experiential Psychotherapy with my clients are the similar growing pains faced by all developing theoretical fields. New approaches struggle to define and justify themselves both to the professionals in their respective field as well as to a skeptical public. A quick review of the historical development of present day psychotherapy illustrates how different theoretical frameworks vie for dominance, acceptance, and respectability. Eventually an emerging field matures to the place where practitioners are able to flow between new and old therapies, theories, and techniques without conflict. I foresee Equine Experiential Psychotherapy evolving in the same manner.

What I have come to believe is that no matter what orientation you bring to psychotherapy, or what certification you achieve, the one variable that has been shown to be critically important is the trusting, respectful, and compassionate relationship that develops between therapist and client, whether the therapist has two or four legs is irrelevant!

Organization of *Beyond Words:*

After I had run a few EEP trainings, I began writing a manual that was to be a flexible agenda for each workshop. That manual grew up into *Beyond Words*.

Beyond Words is divided into three parts. Part One covers the basics of horse/human interactions, basic mindfulness training, and the description of EEP exercises embedded within psychological theory. Part Two explores different clinical populations that are amenable to EEP. Developing appropriate EEP treatment plans based on the underlying condition and specific behavioral goals are reviewed. Part Three covers the technical details necessary for setting up EEP Programs.

My hope is that you will get as much from reading *Beyond Words* as I have from writing it. We are at the beginning of a wonderful journey, our saddlebags are packed, our horses well rested, and off we go.

Introduction

HORSES: THE HEALING MAGIC
OF HONEST CONNECTION

....Horses react to what lies in our hearts, not in our heads. They are not confused by the words we use to lie to ourselves or hide from others.

Alan Hamilton, *Zen Mind, Zen Horse*

Deciding to Heal

We connect with our hearts, but too many people, particularly those of us who have been emotionally wounded, hide out in the sterile but safe world of our intellect. We might not be aware of the fact that we have cut ourselves off from the life sustaining energy of our emotions. We look in the mirror, we talk to our friends, and we travel through our lives, unaware that there is a deeper, richer world available to us.

So much of our sadness, our discontent, our addictions and compulsions are driven by the emptiness we experience when we detach from our emotional selves. We often mistake this emptiness as boredom, anxiety, compulsiveness, hunger, and/or loneliness.

The most powerful and painful disconnection happens to the human heart and soul when we have been traumatized, when we have had our feelings, our basic humanness, negated, ignored or betrayed. We call this "soul murder." Perhaps we were raised in frightening and unstable families, or perhaps we were assaulted, emotionally abandoned, physically threatened, or survived a war powerlessly watching dear friends die. Perhaps we have endured years of physical abuse and intimidation, unable to garner the confidence necessary to flee. In all these instances, the human connection is frayed, destroyed by mistrust, confusion, hurt and brutal inhumanity. Why stick around to feel the pain you cannot escape? It is so much easier to detach, to dissociate, leaving the feeling part of yourself behind, collateral damage in your life.

How do we begin to heal the wounds? How do we begin to feel the pain of the past without being overwhelmed? How do we hold onto hope?

Our hurt was engendered interpersonally; our healing must also be. For that, we borrow from the patience and kindness of horses… as have generations before us. Through our ongoing non-verbal connection with horses, we can begin to regain the trust and belief in our own inherent goodness.

Why Horses

The mystical connection that exists between horses and humans has been documented from time immemorial. From the Greek myth of Chiron, the famous centaur, who was believed to symbolize the positive combination of man's animal and spiritual nature, through American Indians' love and reverence for their horse companions, to our present day fascination with "horse whisperers," people have been enchanted and entranced by the deep relationship between horse and man.

Carl Jung, one of the founding fathers of present day psychotherapy, explored the significance of horses in the Collective Unconscious, that part of our primordial memory hypothesized to be shared universally by all people throughout history. He postulated that the symbol of the horse (archetype) represents the darker, unexplored area of our psyche (our shadow), where our deepest wounds hide from being known. It is through our connection with the dark wisdom of the horse that we are able to bring to light that part of ourselves that we need to be whole.

Little girls risk their first intimate relationships with horses who carry all the hopes, dreams, and longings of the prepubescent child. Soldiers, wounded spiritually, emotionally, and physically from the war, turn to horses for the forgiveness and acceptance that they need to be able to return to their lives. Women gravitate to horses, instinctually captivated by their healing feminine energy. So many people, throughout time, have been drawn to these huge, gentle creatures. These animals have held, and continue to hold, a sacred place in our world.

The space between words is where we live with horses. It is in the silence that we listen the most carefully and are more likely to be truly heard.

The goal of *Beyond Words* is to connect the advances made in the treatment and understanding of mental health issues with the knowledge we have accrued through the years about the nature of horses. My hope is to be able to integrate the two professional worlds of equine specialist and psychotherapist, so that each can appreciate, communicate, and work together in furthering the practice of Equine Experiential Psychotherapy (EEP).

EEP requires intimate teamwork among the equine expert, the psychotherapist, and, of course, the horse for the benefit of the client. It is an intricate dance weaving the three components of this healing triangle with the well-being of the individual and the welfare of the horse always in center stage.

Basic Philosophy

Beyond Words offers equine specialists, psychotherapists, and clients an overview of the ways in which equine experiential psychotherapy can be integrated into the practice of traditional psychotherapy. I have endeavored to employ user-friendly vocabulary and examples so that practitioners from both fields can begin to understand and appreciate the world view of their co-therapists.

There are many excellent models of EEP. The two major approaches that are presently employed in equine experiential therapy are: 1) using a horse as a metaphor/object and 2) using the relationship that develops between horses and human as the basis for healing and growth. Many EEP programs include a hybrid of both. It is the responsibility of the individual practitioner to become familiar with these different paradigms.

I blend the various approaches to EEP in the same manner as I blend various therapeutic techniques in my practice. The skill is knowing when to use what, with whom, and under what conditions and the ability to effortlessly shift directions as necessary.

Well-trained equestrian therapists should be well versed in *all* the various techniques and philosophies within their field of expertise, regardless of their credentialing orientation. Our goal is to be able to address the needs of our clients with whatever intervention works best, not just those we feel comfortable with. Our selection of treatment strategies needs to be as complex and multifaceted as the people we hope to help.

My own bias is towards a more interpersonal approach. Most people's emotional wounds result from significant failures in their relationship history, be it an unavailable mother, an overwhelmed family system, or a betrayal of a trusted person. The list is, unfortunately, endless.

Carl Jung, famous psychotherapist and one of Freud's disciples, wrote about the impressive power of relationships to create change. In medieval times, alchemists believed that the right combinations of elements could change baser metals into gold. Jung, borrowing from this belief, posited that the Alchemical Transformation that occurs when all the elements, in our case, therapists, clients and horses, are willing to engage in an honest and heartfelt manner, is the basis of psychological healing and change.

This does not preclude the use of metaphor and behavioral interventions in equine experiential psychotherapy when appropriate

In sum, equine experiential psychotherapy is a dance performed by the equine specialist, the psychotherapist, the horse, and your client. The dance changes and the steps can get complicated, but if you allow the music to inspire you, you arrive at a different and better place when the music ends.

As we begin this journey, all I ask you to bring with you are your curiosity, your openness to new ideas, and your willingness to try, and try again, and, of course, some water! It can get thirsty on the trail!

PART I

THE BASIS OF EQUINE PSYCHOTHERAPY FROM A PSYCHOLOGICAL PERSPECTIVE

Chapter One

Mindfulness -The Way of the Horse

Let go of the battle. Breathe quietly and let it be. Let your body relax and your heart soften. Open to whatever you experience without fighting.

Jack Kornfield, A *Path With A Heart*

Before we meet the horse, before we even enter the barn, we need to learn how to stay mindful, to be aware of how we are feeling and what we are experiencing in this present moment. Horses live in the here and now; it is the basis of their serenity and survival. Being with them is an invitation to join them in their world.

To practice mindfulness, we begin by breathing. Yes, I know you know how to breathe; you are alive, aren't you? But how alive? All creatures breathe.

Horses are quite expert at deep, heart-felt breathing. They can gently guide us in experiencing the difference between renewing breath, where all senses are attuned to what is going on, versus hurried, Western Breath which just gets you from one place to the next as fast as your little feet can carry you.

It might be helpful to remember that our first breath upon birth is a wonderful intake of life-giving breath, and our last breath, at our passing, is a final exhalation of that same life-breath. How many breathes we have in-between is unknown; how we choose to instill our breath with meaning is up to us.

Harnessing the power of mindfulness

The basis of most Eastern traditions, the possibility of being mindful of the present moment, has seeped into the consciousness of the Western culture. We are usually so busy ruminating over the past or obsessing over the future that we miss out on what's happening *right now* in our lives. Mindfulness enables us to awaken to our life as it exists in this moment.

As I walk along city streets, I notice I am actually leaning forward …so anxious to get to where I am going that I am literally on a tilt. As I am driving, I find myself passing slower cars so that I can lead the pack. I have no idea what the rush is. I just rush.

When I enter a stable, I become aware that my breathing slows down and deepens, my heart quiets, whatever muscle tension I carried into the barn starts to ease, and my thoughts stop racing. I smell the aroma of fresh hay and horses, I hear them moving around in their stalls, I find myself smiling as some of the horses stick their heads out for a quick pat or perhaps, if lucky, a carrot! I notice the softness of their noses as they nuzzle my fingers or the feel of their tongue as they lick my hand hello. I am mindful of the moment. This moment. There is nothing but *this* moment.

Horses model mindfulness. It is where they live every moment of their lives.

Throughout this work, I will be reminding you to breathe, to notice what is happening *right now*. What do you see? What do you feel? Where do you feel it? If you get lost, just notice the horses. Their whole world is contained in the here and now.

EXERCISE: A MAP TO MINDFULNESS...BREATHING

Feelings come and go like clouds in a windy sky. Conscious breathing is my anchor.

Hanh Nhat Thich

This exercise can be used to start and end all therapy sessions. In addition, any time you feel that the client is starting to emotionally escalate, getting more anxious, fearful, angry, and/or stressed, deep breathing can gently bring them back to themselves. It will also help the therapy horse who is probably reacting to the increasing negative emotional energy.

Using your breath will be an integral component in doing equine psychotherapy. You will find that many of the exercises in the manual incorporate mindfulness and breathe work. So let us start now in practicing using breath as a healing and centering instrument.

1. Breathing! Always a good thing. Sit or stand up straight, shoulders back. This gives your lungs room to expand. Take a deep breath through your nose. Let the breath flow effortlessly into you; send the air directly to your belly so that you blow up like a happy Buddha. Now...breathe *slowly* out through your mouth to the count of ten. Try breathing like this for five deep breaths. Attend only to your breathing. Allow all other thoughts to drift away, like clouds across the sky. Wouldn't you like to feel this relaxed more often? Just breathe.

2. Close your eyes and send the breath to your shoulders. Are they up around your ears? Let them drop. You might like to roll your head to release even more hidden tension. Keep going....breathe. Send the breath on a quick trip around your body, check if you are holding tension in your jaw, down your neck, down your back, down your throat, down your arms, down your chest, your belly, your thighs, shins, and your feet.

3. Slowly open your eyes. If everything is a bit fuzzy, good for you! That is the "soft eyes" that trainers are always at you to experience.

4. Now…notice. With your eyes….what do you see? With your nose….what do you smell. With your body…what do you feel? Stay present. Stay grounded. Stay here.

5. Go stand next to your horse. Just relax with him. Perhaps you would like to stroke him, lean on him, nuzzle him, whatever you feel like doing in *this moment*. What do you see when you look at your horse. What do you notice? What do you smell when you sniff him? How does it make you feel? Where do you feel it? How does it feel to stroke him? Lean on him? Nuzzle him? Where do you feel it? Good! Step back and breathe.

It is very difficult and somewhat exhausting to maintain a mindful, present, aware stance. It gets easier! Horses live in this place; it is the world they inhabit.

We will continue to practice being mindful as we go through the rest of the exercises in the manual.

Meeting your horse therapist

Relationships begin the minute we meet each other. Impressions are formed, feelings exchanged, hopes and expectations flower.

In The Barn

We begin our relationship with a horse by grooming him, a time-honored way of establishing connection. It is just the equine friendly thing to do. With horses, it is a lovely ritual practiced with respect for both participants similar to the ancient ritual of sharing tea, a civilized way of getting to know each other. Grooming a horse is also terrific therapy for us humans. It lowers our heart rate, slows down our breathing, allows us to practice being in the here and now, and engages our ancient nurturing instincts.

It is a treat for the horse too since horses love to be pampered. The act of brushing a horse's coat stimulates his body and warms him up for whatever comes next. And all that attention? Can't beat it. It is also the beginning of the bonding experience between you and the horse.

While grooming your horse, try to stay in the moment. Try not to drift away to whatever you were ruminating about on the way to the barn or to what you need to do after your session. I promise, your worries will be waiting patiently for you after you leave the stable.[5]

Look at your horse. Do you think he is dwelling anxiously about what just happened before his grooming? Or what is going to happen next? Nope, he is simply enjoying the attention and sensations of being brushed. Try being here… in this moment. Take in the smells of the horses and the hay, the sounds of the horses stirring and neighing to each other, the softness of the horse's coat under your hand, the silkiness of his mane and coarseness of his tail.

Take time to lose yourself in his big brown eyes. You are now looking into each other, gently and deeply. Stroke the side of his neck and reassure him with the quietness of your voice. It is a special, private moment. Cherish it.

After you finish grooming him, stand back and admire your work. Tell the horse how gorgeous he looks and congratulate yourself for bonding with your new buddy. Your "thank you" will be his looking smug and proud of himself and a happy snort when he sees you next time you come to the stable.

---

[5]   I often invite my client(s) to write down some worry or concern that they're dealing with and leave it at the barn door. There's a "worry" bucket at the entrance to the stable for this purpose. They can either collect their worry as they depart or leave there if they no longer need it!

Grooming: A Tea Ceremony

In the Great Outdoors: Horse Etiquette 101

Yes. That big thing in the field that seems to be ignoring you is a horse. Do not be fooled, he is aware of you. He is attentive to everything around him. That is how he survives. If you are a prey animal, your main defense against predators (let us say a lion) is to run, fast! For a horse, being hyper aware of his immediate environment, being alert to potential danger and startling easy, enables him to survive. However, right now, you do not look like anything that would eat him. Not sensing any need for alarm, he keeps on munching the grass. As long as you keep your gestures and voice quiet and calm, he will be calm, too.

When you go to say hello, you will want to be at about a 45 degree angle from his eyes. He can see you at this angle, so it is only polite to introduce yourself eye to eye. Whenever you approach him, to pet him, groom him, and lead him, etc. say "hello" first. He will remember you. Keep your movements, gestures and voice quiet and relaxed. You might offer the palm of your hand for a quick sniff and/or lick.

Be aware of where your feet are in relation to his hoofs. He will not mean to, but he might accidently step on your foot (or stomp on your foot if he is scaring away flies) and that does not tickle! It is your responsibility to make sure your feet and his feet do not tangle. If you find a horse's hoof on your foot, stay calm, lean into his shoulder and have him move.

When you circle behind a horse, it is always a good idea to have your hand on him so he knows where you are. When you are face to face with his rump, make sure you are either very close to him or about six feet away to avoid getting kicked. Also, always keep a soft chatter going on so that he can place you in space.

Though his nose is very kissable, do not get too close to your buddy's face. He might pick just that moment to look into your eyes…and there goes your chin!

Those are some guidelines for hanging with horses. No matter how cute they are, no matter how much you would like to bundle them in your arms, they are still horses. As brilliant as they are, they are clueless as to their size and weight. We picture horses as these brave, magnificent creatures that charge into battles or jump six story walls, but these are the same creatures that can get spooked by a flapping plastic bag or a puddle. So imagine how spooky you can be if you're not mindful of your actions!

In sum, approach a horse slowly and gently. Remember, we are working on making connections, gaining trust, and establishing mutual respect. They are as cautious of you as you are of them. Real relationships take time.

EXERCISE: CIRCLE YOUR PARTNER

This is an easy, introductory exercise for people who are new to horses. It can also be used as a way of getting a new client, and his therapy horse, to feel comfortable with each other, to pick up each other's smell, energy, touch, etc.

1. As the name implies, simply circle around the horse keeping physical contact with him at all times. Gentle murmuring of sweet-nothings can be added on, always a nice technique for developing new relationships!

2. At first, you can have the horse on a lead line. As the relationship progresses, you can quietly call for the horse to come to you and, with supervision, practice circling with the horse at liberty (not on a lead line).

3. In both cases, talk about what you were feeling and what you thought the horse might be feeling. This might also open up a discussion on horse body language….how do you *know* what a horse is feeling? He isn't exactly going to tell you!

EXERCISE: MEET AND GREET – DEVELOPING TRUST

This exercise can be become part of the routine at the beginning of each session. It is a gentle invitation to begin the nonverbal give and take that characterizes the horse/human relationship. It can also be added whenever things get a little chaotic. You are always welcome to stop any exercise at any point and have the horse and client get centered by repeating this gentle nose bump.

1. Breathe deeply and quietly. Get centered. Scan your body for any areas of tension, open up your shoulders and expose your heart area.

2. Stand about a foot away from your horse, slightly to the right or left of his head. Now wait for him to notice or approach you. Imagine your heart is open and available. The more vulnerable you are, the more of an invitation

for your horse to step forward and say "hello." You might offer him your fist for him to sniff. Fists look like noses to horses; who nose why?

3. Or, if your horse is very shy, it is okay to approach him. Remember, walk to the right or left of his field of vision. Slowly raise your arm to stroke his neck; too fast and he will startle and jerk backwards. Talk about rejection! When you think he's ready, offer him your fist to sniff.

4. Step back, releasing the tension which is a reward for a horse.[6] Remember, first dates are always a bit stressful!

Greeting…A Nose Bump

---

[6]   Releasing tension on the horse is very rewarding to them; it relaxes them. Even shifting your gaze away from them is felt as a release of tension!

During this exercise, a recent patient felt terribly rejected and sad. The horse came to greet every other participant but avoided her. She is a very sweet, kind, somewhat shy woman. Knowing that she had been sexually abused and unprotected as a child, it was not surprising that she responded, "Terrified!" when asked how she felt when the large horse started to approach her. She realized that she felt safe approaching others, but became alarmed when someone she wasn't familiar with, approached her.

She came to understand that her tendency to shy away from people had left her alone and lonely. After practicing some grounding and safety techniques, she visualized opening her heart to the horse. Sure enough, the horse came right to her and gave her a lovely nuzzle. And the horse, who also had a rocky start to life, followed her around for the rest of the session; they had discovered kindred spirits!

We will continue to practice being mindful as we go through the rest of the exercises in the manual.

In Chapter One we examine the ancient wisdom associated with mindfulness and breathing and how we can take this into our hectic and stress strewn lives. Being from a Western culture, it is quite a challenge to slow down enough to give ourselves an opportunity to simply breath. The importance of being mindful of what's happening in your life, right at this precise moment, is discussed and practiced.

The horse, as healer, is introduced and basic barn and horse etiquette is reviewed. And so we begin our journey. Saddle up.

Chapter Two

Horses & Humans: Building Healthy Connections

Real friendship, love, and connectedness thrive only if respect and safety comes first.

Let's begin with the concept of boundaries. Boundaries are the physical distance we maintain around us that keep us feeling safe and unviolated. Each individual has an invisible space that surrounds them. Part of being an emotionally related human being is to be able recognize and respect others' boundaries…as well as your own.[7] That means being able to pick up subtle, nonverbal cues as to how physically close you can come to another person without causing discomfort. When a country's boundaries are violated, it is considered an act of aggression. We experience it in the same manner.

Boundaries can also be emotional, how comfortable we are with letting people get close to us. It is our way of protecting our privacy. "This is as much information as I am willing to share with you, until I learn to trust you." Each of us, as a result of events that have happened in our lives, has different levels of tolerance and conditions for emotional closeness and intimacy.

---

[7] Different cultures have varying degrees of distance with which they are comfortable. Americans, not surprisingly, have a need for a wide boundary. Perhaps you have experienced people who innocently stand too close for comfort; that might be their cultural norm.

People sometimes think that setting limits on what they will and will not do is perceived as a hostile act, that people will not like them if they establish and protect their boundaries. These people tend to get "run over" by other people's needs and desires. Perhaps they have come to believe that it is better to constantly give in than to be alone and abandoned, as if it is an either/or choice.

Horses also need their boundaries respected. A horse that has been abused, violently trained, or abandoned will require time and patience to be able to trust others not to hurt him. In time, with enough consistency and caring, even a very mistrustful horse will begin to trust and let you near him. In that, we are not so very different.

Most horses will take some time to warm to you, to learn that you are a friend. Until that time, it requires patience, kindness, and persistence to develop trust. So keep your distance, until invited in!

HORSE BOUNDARY EXERCISES

You will learn that setting clear boundaries, taking care of yourself, does not threaten abandonment or evoke anger. To do this effectively, you need to be aware of your own personal boundaries, to come to know what makes you comfortable and when you feel violated.

EXERCISE: HORSEY DOSEY DOE

This exercise can be used in any situation where boundary violation has been an issue. Some examples might be: any physical abuse, incest, rape, spousal abuse, being the victim of any violent crime, and/or being in a family characterized by alcohol or drug abuse.

1. Pair off with a human. One of you stands still; the other moves toward you sloooowly. Notice when the closeness begins to feel intrusive. Raise your hand to signal your discomfort. Your partner takes a *breath/step* back (step back one step and breathe out deeply and gently). Approach again, repeating,

until you both get close enough for a head bump (literally). Let us bump heads gently, shall we?

2. Pick out a horse in the field and practice dosey-doeing with him. With a gentle outstretched fist (pathetically mimicking a horse nose) move slooowly toward your horsey partner. Wait until the horse either turns and acknowledges your "hello" or actually gives you a nice bump on the nose/fist back.

3. Slowly rock back with a calm, deep breath, releasing tension. You are checking out each other's boundaries and respectfully giving distance if one or the other of you shows any discomfort. Perhaps the horse shies away from you; step back and give him more space. Or if the horse comes too close for comfort, feel free to back up or nudge him back with your hand on his nose.

4. Now, let's try to dance. Invite your horse to move towards you by presenting your fist for a nose bump. Remember to open your heart. Once your partner comes forward, take another gentle step back, again inviting him forward. And off you go! The famous and well known Horse Trot (foxes are so passé).

ENERGY FIELDS AND BOUNDARIES

When horses are grazing and one horse senses danger, all the horses pick up the survival cue and begin to run from the possible predator. How do they communicate this warning to each other? They do not make a sound; that would be counterproductive since it would alert the predator as to their location. The alarm is transmitted….how? We assume that it is their exceptional sensitivity to each other, their bio-energetic field, that transmits important information.

Horses generate a tremendous amount of energy, particularly around their chest/heart area. A powerful way to connect with a horse is to enter their field of energy, always asking permission to go deeper as you get closer. Three to five inches from the horse is an optimal distance to stop. Once there, treat both of you to a calming energy massage.

Energy healing is as old as the history of man. There are a multitude of theories and beliefs about its source, efficacy, and spirituality. What we do know, horses and those of us who bond with them, is that energy connects us on a deeper, more intimate, truthful level and isn't that we all long for in our lives?

EXERCISE: "CON SU PERMISSO" (With Your Permission)

Thanks to Barbara Rector, founder of Adventures in Awareness (AIA)

As with Horse Dosey Do, this exercise is excellent for learning to feel and respect boundaries and can be used with any client population. It is also a wonderful way to learn about the energy and sensitivity of horses. Con Su Permisso could also be incorporated as part of the "greeting" part at the beginning of each session, a respectful way of welcoming each other.

1. First, center. Breathe deeply. Send the breath down through your body and relax. Now rub your hands together, gently, and breathe into them. You are localizing your own energy this way.
2. Slooowly approach the horse, palms raised and facing the horse. Experience the first energy field. It will feel like a slight resistance, as if you are walking through waves. Move through the energy field into the next and the following one, until you are about six inches from the horse. People report that the energy field feels like a tingling or warmth in their palms.
3. Then, without actually touching him, begin to massage his body from a distance of about three inches. Feel what areas on his body pulsate with stronger fields. You will probably notice that his heart area sends out very strong energy pulses, stronger than the rest of his body. Most horses love this massage! (Weird as this may seem).
4. When you feel complete, just step back. You might want to say "thank you" to the horse for allowing you to come so close to him. It requires trust and honesty to deeply connect with a horse.

Con Su Permisso- With Your Permission

The Power Of The Heart

GETTING YOUR NEEDS MET – A CORE COMPONENT OF HEALTHY RELATIONSHIPS

Each of us has developed a repertoire of behaviors for interacting with other people. Included in this, is the ability to know what you need and effectively communicate your desires to those closest to you. Some communication styles are more effective in achieving your goals than others. Of the following three major communication styles, which one best describes you? (Of course, there is overlap and different people and situations elicit different responses from each of us. However, we tend to prefer one method over another.)

Passive Aggressive Style: If you tend to be passive aggressive, your goal is to express your anger and annoyance without taking responsibility for it. You avoid the risk of having people respond in kind to your anger. You *hate* confrontations.

Under this category, we can put "mind reading." If someone cared enough about you, they should *know* what you want, need, and are annoyed about without you having to say! This way you can be righteously angry without having to hazard expressing your needs.

Your lack of courage makes you infuriating to others. You might:

1. Be chronically late for any appointment with that "uncaring" person, each time having a "legitimate" excuse.
2. Intentionally misinterpret an important assignment because you are annoyed at your boss for some unacknowledged slight.
3. Be dependably disappointed in any gift your insensitive boyfriend attempts to give you.

Aggressive Style: Motivated by a deep and unacknowledged insecurity, you bully your way through life and people. No one stands in your way! You do not ask, you demand. You find opportunities to be sarcastic and belittling. You are opinionated, condescending and hostile. Your intimidation alienates everyone around you. You might:

1. Demand that your staff stay late on Friday just because you can.
2. Physically push your wife away when you do not like how she is stacking the dishwasher.
3. Take every opportunity to yell at waiters who do not jump to attention when you want something, NOW! Show them you are in control by leaving a miserable tip.

You probably are aware of your tyrannical behavior. People might listen to you, but they surely do not like you.

Assertive Style: You respect other people's time, space, and desires. You *ask* for what you want and need in a clear, direct and respectful manner. You quickly try to clear up any hurt or confusion, taking responsibility for your part in misunderstandings. You actually take the garbage out without being hounded to do so. Your clarity leads people to respond to your requests positively. You might:

1. Check with other people before you take actions that will affect them.
2. Seek clarification and understanding when a request is not fully understood.
3. Clearly state that something is urgent or important to you in a respectful but strong manner.

People love being with you. You provide a safe, calm, encouraging, environment.

- Which category mostly describes your interpersonal style?
- What steps can you take to change a passive/aggressive or aggressive style?
- How do you think these three styles are going to affect the way you get along with your horse?

GROUP EXERCISE: RECOGNIZING YOUR COMMUNICATION STYLE

This exercise is one of a number which helps the client learn about themselves "in action." The horse is a wonderful, if not humbling, teacher in that he is highly responsive to the tone, mannerism and emotional noise each person brings to the task.

1. As a group, head out to the paddock. Each person will have an opportunity to role play each interpersonal style with a horse. Both you and the group can take note of the horse's response to each style.

First ask the horse to move in a passive-aggressive style. This would probably be indirect with a touch of underlying hostility. Then ask for the horse to move in an aggressive, demanding manner. Lastly, request that the horse moves in an assertive manner, making clear your desire without coercing the horse's compliance. Remember to reward the horse for any effort by releasing pressure.

2. Regroup and discuss what you experienced.

What style was the most comfortable for you? Which the least? Could you benefit from balancing your responses? How do you think this would make a difference in your everyday dealing with the people in your life?

In Chapter Two the process of building a relationship with your horse, based on mutual respect and understanding, is examined. The need to set clear boundaries and effectively communicate your needs is put in motion as you practice developing your human/equine relationship.

Trotting onto feelings!

Chapter Three

Adding in Feelings

Developing the unique relationships between human and horse…provides vivid proof that our emotions are felt by and matter to others.

Linda Kohanov, *The Tao of Equus*

THE NATURE OF FEELING

What we *think* is often worlds away from what we *feel*. People in our modern world tend to over-rely on thinking thereby diminishing the rich information offered by our emotions. We cut ourselves off at the neck, dividing our bodies from our minds, as if we are two separate entities. Sadly, many of us remain unaware of this split. Horses have a wonderful way of guiding us gently back to our emotion selves.

WHAT EXACTLY *IS* FEELING?

When discussing feelings, we are actually talking about three different realms of experiences: Cognitive (our thoughts), Affect (our emotions), and Soma (how our emotions are experienced in our bodies).

HUMAN INFORMATION PROCESSING

Our brains process incoming information in a manner similar to computers (and vice versa). Data received via our senses gets inputted into our system triggering many diverse mechanisms in our bodies. Eventually, the data gets transmitted to our neocortex where meaning and significance gets assigned.

For example, we *hear* a loud noise and startle. This triggers our adrenalin to start pumping and our heart rates to accelerate. We *feel* anxious. We look around to ascertain where the noise is coming from and *see* a speeding motorcycle heading down the street. Our neocortex has assigned meaning to the incoming stimuli. The noise is caused by the motorcycle.

The human neocortex, which is highly advanced compared to that of other living creatures, is responsible for making sense of this onslaught of incoming information. Based on the meaning we have assigned to the noise, we *decide* not to cross until the motorcycle is way down the road. All systems relax, and we go back to whatever we were doing.

Because horses have a small neocortex, their primary way of responding to the world is mostly emotionally and physically. They survive, as do all prey animals, by quickly reacting to any perceived danger in the environment. If something feels threatening, they do not slow down to assess the situation; by that time, they would surely have been eaten! For example, the lead horse senses danger in the vicinity, perhaps a huge, unknown entity that had not been in the field this morning has frighteningly appeared. He alerts his herd to the danger and they take off running. Once the horses feel safe, their breathing returns to normal, their bodies relax, etc., they might return and explore the new tractor which has suddenly materialized in the corner of the barn. Danger over, they go back to what they most love doing… grazing!

It is almost magical to see how horses communicate their feelings silently to each other through an invisible energy field. (This energy is what we experienced when we practiced "Con Su Permisso.") If one horse, usually whoever is the head male or female, senses danger, they are able to convey the impending threat to the rest of the herd without uttering a sound. To make noise would be to alert the predator of the horses' presence. The herd, in turn, is primed to run and to follow the lead horse to safety. Once the threat has passed, the dominant horse relaxes his body and the rest of the herd follows.

Here is another example of the difference between human and equine feelings. Let us say a storm is approaching. We can hear the far away sound of thunder and attribute the noise to the approaching storm (cognitive appraisal). We can feel the wind pick up and see the sky darkening (somatic appraisal), and we might feel a bit alarmed by the prospect of the impending storm (emotional). We then decide, based on this information, to head home for safety.

A horse hears the thunder, gets nervous, and runs!

EXERCISE: THE WHAT, WHERE, AND HOW OF FEELINGS

The following is a basic primer on the differences between cognitive (thinking), versus emotions (feeling), versus somatic (body) responses. It is important that the client understand the distinctions between these ways of processing information. Needless to say, when working with our horse co-therapists, we will be tuning into their emotional and somatic responses as well as our clients.

You can refer to these different modes of processing information at any time. It takes a while for people to get the hang of this; we have spent so much of our human lives living in the cognitive realm! Asked how they feel, more often than not people will tell you what they think. So, if asked, "How did it feel when the horse came towards you?" A classic response would be, "I felt that she must really like me!" "Well, that's great, but that's a thought not a feeling." "OK, it made me feel happy and warm." "Where did you feel it?" "In my heart and my belly." "Good!"

Examine your experiences with feelings by asking yourself these questions:

1. Sitting in the barn with this manual:

What are you thinking? (Cognitive) "I didn't show up to this workshop to stare at horses and read manuals!"

What are you feeling? (Emotional) "I'm feeling annoyed, bored, irritated, and anxious."

Where do you feel these emotions? (Somatic) "My head aches, my stomach is clenched, and my foot is tapping the floor in an irritated fashion."

2. After meeting the horse:

What are you thinking? "The horse doesn't like me. He greeted everyone but me."

How are you feeling? "I'm feeling rejected, embarrassed, sad, and alone."

Where do you feel your feelings? My face is turning red, my eyes are tearing up, and my shoulders are slumping.

3. After grooming and massaging the horse:

What do you think the horse is thinking? "Not much."

What do you think your horse is feeling? "Content, safe, secure, calm."

What are you feeling right now? "Content, calm."

How is the horse communicating how he is feeling? "His head is relaxed and down, his ears are pointed forward, his mouth is doing that gobbly thing he does when he's happy and chatty, his breathing is nice and slow."

How are you communicating to yourself what you are feeling? "My breathing is relaxed, my shoulders are down where they should be, my forehead is smooth, my hands are unclenched, and I'm smiling!"

Try this exercise in your group. Each person gets a chance to talk about what they are thinking and feeling and where, in their body, that experience is felt. If someone is stuck, you can help out by describing how you are experiencing your colleague in that moment using his or her somatic cues.

The Horse's Turn: How is *he* feeling?

Horses have a repertoire of emotional responses that basically include fear/anxiety, anger, happiness, sadness, and contentment. They express these emotions through their bodies and the sounds they emanate. You can learn your horse's emotional response pretty quickly. Taking time to observe your horse in his natural setting will yield wonderful insight.

Perhaps your mare is grouchy and in no mood to tolerate the other horses' shenanigans. Her ears go back when they encroach on her territory, her tail starts to swish, she makes a menacing noise, she might stamp her foot, and if that is not enough to keep the pesky ponies out of her way, she might give them an emphatic bite. If, later in the day, she is feeling calm and playful, she might meander over to the other horses, see what is going on, share a bundle of hay, and give a nudge to see if anyone wants to play "who moves whom." Her ears will be up and alert, her tail relaxed (except to swat away flies), and she might give a neighborly neigh to say hello to her buddies

But before you start to psychoanalyze your horse, realize that there is another common human processing error: to "project" your unwanted, unacknowledged feelings onto others, in this case the innocent horse. "Boy, that horse looks sad!" No, his head is down because he is relaxing. He is basically content, having just eaten and been brushed. Are *you* feeling sad?

I remember the first time I was in a horse stable as a grown-up (12 year old camp experiences do not count!). I looked at the row of horses in their stalls looking at me; they all looked so angry! Every one of them. I asked my companion, an experienced horse person, if all horses were grouchy? She reassured me that the horses were perfectly content. In hindsight, I realized I was "projecting" my feelings onto the horses. I was not at all aware of my pervasive anger at the time; in fact I was having a great time. But the anger was there, waiting for me.

EXERCISE: WHO'S FEELING WHAT ABOUT WHOM? The Power of Projection

This is a wonderful exercise to learn, first hand, about our tendency to 'project' our feelings onto others rendering communication, the basis of intimacy, a very complicated, confusing endeavor! Feel free to use this exercise whenever you perceive someone projecting, instead of owning, their feelings.

1. The group chooses one horse in the field.
2. Write down what you think the horse is feeling.
    What clues do you have?
3. Write down what *you* are thinking and feeling.
4. Share both thoughts and feelings with the group and discuss.

What would you gain by being honest with yourself and risking, acknowledging and expressing your absolutely human needs and emotions?

Emotional Contagion

A corollary to emotional projection is emotional contagion. Often we are unaware of how our feelings get transmitted to the people and horses around us. Are we projecting our feelings or are we innocently transmitting them to everyone in our immediate environment? Have you ever walked into a room and felt the tension in the air? Perhaps having walked in on a marital spat? Uncomfortable! In the same way, we can innocently bring our bad mood into the barn with us. The horses might seem particularly antsy that day. Is it that the horses are picking up on our negative energy or are we projecting our grouchiness onto the horses? It is often difficult to differentiate.

This could also work the other way. If you are in a happy, energized mood, you might find yourself dealing with a playful, bucking, animated horse. Could be fun for both of you, if you are prepared for horsing around.

Once we learn to recognize our emotions, we can take responsibility for them and "take ownership" of the energy we are transmitting into the environment. Before entering the barn, you can go through a "feelings checklist" to determine what emotional noise you might innocently be dragging in. Imagine the Peanut character Linus, but instead of walking around in a cloud of dirt, you're walking around in a cloud of feelings.

I have come to realize that my natural playfulness around Remi, my therapy horse, is contagious. One individual, who later reported being "near to terror" at the thought of even being near a horse, told me that she "picked up" my happy, confident energy around Remi and was able to relax in turn. Similar to countertransference, we therapists need to take ownership of our own feelings during sessions so we know whose emotions we are *actually* dealing with.

A Caveat About Feelings

Working with feelings is the core of our work. Acknowledging and listening to our feelings gives us vital information about ourselves. Now comes the contradictory part. Love your feelings. Make friends with your feelings. Protect your feelings. HOWEVER do not let them drive the car! They are feelings, precious and informative. Strap them next to you, make sure they feel safe, but let your intellect make the major life decisions.

Here is an example. Remember that song from South Pacific, "Some enchanted evening, you might see a stranger across a crowded room," Do NOT run to his side! Run the other way, quickly! Even though your heart might be throbbing, as if you finally met your soul mate, more often than not these immediate attractions are disastrous. Often times we are attracted to people who seem familiar to us; who feel like home. But "home" might not have been the sanest, kindest place in the world. Pull in the reins and slow down. Model horse wisdom and take time to get a sense of this other creature to determine if they are safe, honest, dependable, and emotionally congruent.

Another example from our popular culture is Nancy's song in Oliver Twist. Her boyfriend is a horror. He is physically abusive and cruel. And she knows this, intellectually. Yet she sings, "As long as he needs me, I know where I must be." Well, he kills her. She listened to her "heart" not her head. We do not have the brilliant intuition of horses, we are not prey animals. No horse would have allowed this brute to get anywhere near him.

In sum, both humans and horses are feeling animals, driven by our needs for safety and dependability, drawn to our respective herds for companionship and security. Horses, unlike humans, do not mask or camouflage their feelings. It is a matter of survival for them to be able to quickly pick up clear emotional information. We need to allow our horse therapists to mirror us and in that humble reflection of our true selves, strive for honesty.

THE IMPORTANCE OF BEING EMOTIONALLY CONGRUENT
(*OR IF YOU'RE NOT SURE WHAT YOU'RE FEELING, ASK A HORSE!*)

Horses are exceptionally honest and expect the same of those around them. They will let you know, by their responses, if they experience you as emotionally present *or* if you are masking your true feelings. If you are aware and accepting of what you're feeling, the horse will enjoy your company. If, instead, you are acting as if everything is hunky-dory when in truth you are falling apart, the horse will get confused by all the different messages and take off. Horses can help us get honest about what we are actually feeling.

Meeting a horse for the first time can elicit lots of interesting feelings. You could be scared. Who wouldn't be meeting a huge, powerful animal? Or curious. The horse is just as curious about you as you are about him! Feel unsure about your safety around such a big animal. He feels the same about you. I promise. You will come to realize that they are the biggest babies and have no concept of their size or strength.

Now that you are beginning to recognize and own your feelings, how effective are you in clearly expressing them?

Being congruent, having your feelings and your expression of them match, is essential for effective communication. Your body, facial expression, tone of voice – all must match your message. For example, if you are angry, it is not effective to articulate your annoyance as you giggle and blush. No one will take you seriously. Or if you are scared, let's say of that horse directly in front of you, you will not get the warmth and reassurance you need if you act blustery and loud.

Women, in general, have a particularly hard time acknowledging and expressing negative emotions such as anger, annoyance, and frustration. They try to assert their needs *while at the same time* minimizing the power of their words by nonverbal behaviors. How many of you find yourself blushing and smiling while attempting to express justified anger? Or forgiving or "understanding" why you are not getting your needs met instead of literally standing your ground. How many of you can actually recognize when you have been emotionally hurt and be able to effectively communicate that "ouch?" What makes this such a scary endeavor?

Men often have a difficult time with the "softer" emotions such as hurt, grief, and sorrow. They will hide their emotions, often from themselves as well as everyone else, by staying very busy with multiple projects and/or using numbing behavior, e.g. T.V., computers, and drinking too much. Often times, men will experience their sadness and fear as anger and rage. It is pretty hard to have your needs for comfort, nurturance, and reassurance met when you are screaming at someone. Not effective

Being congruent means standing behind your feelings courageously. "I'm angry!" "You hurt me!" "I need this!" "You can't do this to me!" What do you fear would happen if you assert yourself clearly? Will people not like you? Will they reject you? Will you come across as a controlling bitch? Will you be fired? Rejected? Abandoned?

What if you were to risk saying to someone, "I'm hurting." "I'm ashamed." "I failed." "I'm scared." Will people think you a pathetic wimp? Not up to the job? Would you end up more alone and isolated than you already feel?

What would you gain by being honest with yourself and risk acknowledging and expressing your absolutely human feelings?

Discordant emotions are very confusing and frustrating for horses as well. They are totally dependent on our tones and body language since that is their only means of communicating with us. If we are feeling one way (scared) but acting cocky, a horse might well become anxious and agitated being unsure of which signal to respond to. The fear? That means he should run. The anger? He sense dangers and back away. The meekness? He remains clueless and directionless, which might frighten the horse since there is no one is in charge to protect him. Horses are picking up your scrambled emotions even if you are not.

Horses assess whether the animals (in this case, us) around them are safe by responding to the emotions we emanate, in the same way they do when picking up the emotional energy radiating from other horses. It is irrelevant to them if the emotion is fear, anxiety, joy, or sadness as long as the emotion is clear.

If you risk becoming honest about your emotions, a) the horse will relax and b) you can take steps to calm yourself down by breathing deeply. The horse will mirror you, his breathing will slow, and he will settle down and come say hello. Talk about instant feedback!

Horses are wonderful barometers of honesty. Their responses will help you realize how aware you are, or how cut off you have become, from your own feelings. The closer you get to experiencing and congruently expressing your own feelings, the more trusting the horse will feel in your presence and the more amendable to coming forward at your request. Horses can be gentle and patient teachers. Your avoidance of your feeling was born of ancient fears and wounds. Give yourself the gift of healing, of being here for your life as it enfolds for you.

In sum, horses will let you know if you are being emotionally congruent or not. If you come across aggressively, either the horse will back away or will respond in an aggressive nature to what he might perceive as your challenge. If you come across passively, you will be pushed around by the horses who love to play "Who moves whom." They surely will not listen to you! If you come across jumpy and agitated, your horse will respond in kind and you will be dealing with two jumpy, agitated creatures!

EXERCISE: RISKING HONESTY

This exercise is very similar to the one we discussed for practicing communication styles. They can be used interchangeably. Again, any role playing with horses is a powerful means of learning your impact on another, but with safe, forgiving partners.

1. Practice setting up hypothetical situations that require honest, clear communications. This exercise can be done as role play with the group. Here are some examples:
   - Asking for a raise from an intimidating boss.
   - Insisting that your mate stop belittling you at parties.
   - Sharing with your significant other your feelings of fear and shame.
   - Telling someone that you need them.
   - Requesting a hug.

Alita H. Buzel

How did this exercise feel? Can you imagine areas and times in your life when being congruent can work for you? It is always more effective to clearly communicate what you are feeling as opposed to barking at people or requiring them to read your mind and being hurt when they can't.

Discuss how this felt with the group. What part was most difficult for you? What did you feel? Where did you feel it? What do you need to bring into the world with you to make it safe to express honest emotions?

Next, try getting a horse to follow a command while at the same time giving him mixed messages. For example:

1. Ask your horse to "move on" in a passive, indecisive way. What happens? What does the horse do? Where are his ears? Is he even listening to you? How do you feel about this?
2. Now, try it again using your voice, your body, and your expression to communicate "move on" in a forceful but respectful manner. What does the horse do? Does the horse hate you? Does he never want to speak to you again? I doubt it; he actually appreciates knowing what you want.

In Chapter Three we covered the complexity of feelings and the importance of recognizing and taking ownership of our emotions. The differences between cognitive, emotional, and somatic processing were discussed as well as the effects of emotional incongruity and emotional contagion. All the above is interwoven with our work with horses.

Let's transition to Trauma.

Chapter Four

Understanding the Power of Trauma

Experiencing the violation and horror of trauma, humans can become like prey animals, ready to run or in a constant state of hyper vigilance or mistrust. Fear...is one of the most ancient emotional energies shared by horses and humans....which tell creatures that their safety is threatened.

Linda Kohanov, *The Tao of Equus*

When we talk about psychological trauma, as opposed to physical trauma, we are addressing the emotional shock and distress caused by experiencing a disastrous event outside the range *of normal human experience*. Examples of psychological trauma could be rape, combat, plane or car crashes, wars, being the victim of a violent crime, being raised in a frightening household, and so on. In our day and age, it could be a terrorist attack which either directly affected you or someone you love; timely examples might be 9/11 or the Boston Marathon bombing.

The trauma could have happened decades ago. Maybe you were abused as a child, witnessed a parent being battered, or served in Viet Nam. It could be ongoing as in spousal abuse, or in the very recent past, for instance, veterans returning from the Mid-East wars zones. With emotional trauma, when it happened often makes little difference in the emotional pain and turmoil it continues to inflict. One of the characteristics of trauma memory, as opposed to regular memory, is that it seems to freeze the event in time so that it always feels as if it's happening *right now* as opposed to in the past.

SNAGS IN INFORMATION PROCESSING DUE TO TRAUMA

Traumatic Memories: To understand the emotional effects of trauma, we have to review a bit about how memories are processed in the brain. Memory formation is a complex and fascinating process that we are just beginning to understand. *If everything goes right, a memory eventually gets stored in long-term memory and can be evoked upon being cued by an event or by simply recalling it. If you want to remember what you did last weekend, you would simply call up that memory, and voila, there it is. Or you might pass the restaurant you ate at and remember what a great (or not so great) meal you had.

However, if something traumatic happens to you, the memory of that horrifying event often fails to be processed in a normal manner. Trauma memories get stuck; they are not metabolized in a way that enables them to enter long term memory store. When a trauma memory gets triggered, it feels as if the actual event is unfolding *right this moment*, with all the terror and pain of the original incident and resultant fight/flight adrenalin flooding. We call these events *flashbacks*. A flashback might be triggered, for example, by a car backfiring causing a war veteran to drop to the ground believing he is, once again, under attack. Or the sound of a plane overhead might cause panic in a person who survived the 9/11 attacks. A particular smell, say pine trees, can generate horror in someone who was raped in the forest as a child. These memories return, full force and unprocessed. They are terrorizing, disorienting, and debilitating. This is the basis for what we know as Post Traumatic Stress Disorder.

People who have been traumatized become hyper-vigilant, scanning their immediate environment for signs of impending danger. They tend to startle easily, as do horses, spooking at objects and events that others assume are harmless. *Survival is first and foremost for prey animals such as horses and for people who have been preyed upon.*

Beyond Words: The Healing Power of Horses

<u>Neuroplasticity:</u> Neurologists have discovered that the brain is capable of rewiring its neural networks. This "neuroplasticity" enables new pathways to be implanted thereby enabling healthier, more adaptive, responses to incoming stimuli. The importance of this to trauma is obvious.

The more any creature (yes, you and the big fellow next to you) has opportunities to experience frightening stimuli and learn to master more effective ways of responding, the more new neural pathways will be formed and deepened. It is similar to laying down railroad tracks...of course it takes a lot of practice for the motorman to automatically take the new, unfamiliar route. One of the major goals of trauma therapy is to lay down new neural pathways that will enable the traumatized person to gain access to more life-promoting strategies. We have found that working with horses has proven highly effective in facilitating just this sort of rewiring.

To understand the theory of neuroplasticity, it is important to have a basic understanding of brain functioning.

NEOCORTEX VERSUS LIMBIC SYSTEM PROCESSING

<u>The Neocortex:</u> The neocortex is responsible for higher-order cognitive processing. Man has the most highly developed neocortex of all animals. This area of the brain is responsible for reasoning and problem-solving as well as attributing meaning and context to our experiences. We hear a sudden noise; we startle, *then* quickly remember that it is the 4th of July, and decide the noise is probably fireworks. That is our neocortex at work.

Horses are sweethearts, but their neocortex is pretty unimpressive. As with all prey animals, they are wired to ensure survival which is reflected in their highly developed limbic system, a *sub*cortical area of the brain.

<u>The Limbic System:</u> The limbic system is the area of the brain responsible for the basic emotions and memories that ensure the continuation of a species. The parts of the limbic system we need to address are the amygdala and the hippocampus.

<u>The Amygdala</u>: The amygdala is one of the primary components of the limbic system. It is responsible for triggering an immediate response if the organism is in perceived danger. The amygdala's "method of comparison is associative" states Daniel Goldman. "When one key element of a present situation is similar to the past, it can call it a 'match"….it (the amygdala) acts before there is full confirmation (that the organism is in actual peril). It frantically commands that we react to the present in ways that were imprinted long ago, with thoughts, emotions, reactions learned in response to events perhaps only dimly similar but close enough to alarm the amygdala."[8]

It follows that prey animals, such as horses, have much larger amygdalae than predatory animals like humans.

<u>The Hypothalamus</u>: The hypothalamus is often referred to as the "command center." Once the amygdala sends a distress signal to the hypothalamus, it pumps epinephrine (adrenalin) into the nervous system triggering a fight/flight response. Anyone who has ever felt a rush of anxiety or been on a horse that unexpectedly spooks, has experienced the surge of adrenalin resulting in shortness of breath, pumping heart, sweating, light headedness, and all sorts of otherwise unpleasant, but fleeting, feelings

<u>Amygdala Hijack</u>: When traumatized individuals are triggered by an object or event that is associated with their trauma, their nervous system responds *as if* they were in imminent danger. Daniel Goldman, in his excellent book, *Emotional Intelligence*, labels this hard wired event, "amygdala hijack." With an amygdala hijack, there is no opportunity for the brain to slow down the response, to associate meaning to the stimuli, and to make the rational decision whether there is truly reason to panic.

For example a veteran is triggered by something that reminds him of the war, such as fireworks on the 4th of July. They could easily mistake the noise as an exploding IED (Improvised Explosive Devise) eliciting a limbic system response. A series

---

[8]   Goldman, Daniel. Emotional Intelligence, pg. 21

of physiological reactions, meant to ensure survival, automatically occur and the individual becomes primed to flee or fight. Horses, being prey animals, are always on the lookout for predators. Their heightened response to danger has enabled them to survive as a species. In fact, it is believed horses have the largest amygdala of all domestic animals. When something alarms them, an instinctive fear response takes over driven by the amygdala. It does not matter if it is a lion near the watering hole or the unfamiliar trailer parked next to the paddock; the reaction might well be panic. Our brave horses, being spooked, turn and run from the perceived threat. Maybe later, once they have not been eaten and they return to their normal state of calm, their natural curiosity leads them to explore the new trailer.

Hyper and Hypo Arousal:[9] When the alarm system of our brain signals "danger!" the limbic system can elicit what appears to be two very contradictory responses in terms of nervous system arousal.

Hyper arousal is a *biological response* to danger. The body is being flooded with adrenalin, the fight or flight hormone, causing heart racing, shallow breathing, sweating, stomach churning, and the feeling we label "panic." The choice is to fight the predator/enemy or to run. Horses prefer to run; they are made for speed. Human response depends on the person, the circumstance, and the automatic assessment of survival possibilities. It is also determined by our trauma history; whether we respond instinctually via the limbic system or whether the information gets processed by the neocortex.

You can see the limbic response in action when your horse is startled by a deer jumping in front of him, a puddle with a strange reflection (his!), an overhead plane roaring or an unknown dog getting too close. And off he goes….with you on his back! This is an example of hyper-arousal. You might experience it, depending on your past history, when a car backfires in a dangerous neighborhood, when your horse starts to rear unexpectedly, or when you are given a surprise quiz.

---

[9]   We will discuss hypo arousal when we talk about the emotional responses to trauma and stress.

In all the above cases, the remedy is to lower the physiological response by *calming your body down*. And we calm down by…breathing! When you stop panicking, when your body relaxes, you might feel a bit tired and shaky, but you will no longer be on full alert. That is why it is so important to learn to center and breathe.

Remember, feelings are contagious. If either you or your horse begins to get agitated, both of you will feel it and respond accordingly. So too, if you sense your horse getting nervous, perhaps there is a new dog approaching, you can calm him down by deep breathing, gently stroking his withers, and keeping your voice low and reassuring. Your calmness will reassure him that someone's in charge and he is safe.

THE POWER OF BREATHING - REVISITED

Horses have an instinct to provide regulation and comfort to herd members in distress; the saying is that the herd only as strong as their weakest member…they sense the breath… deep, low breathing signals relaxation and well being; shallow, fast breathing means danger or discomfort. They exchange information through the breath.

Linda Kohanov, *The Tao of Equus*

In any animal, when the amygdala has been triggered, a series of somatic responses follow that are meant to prepare the body to fight or flee. Some of the symptoms include a racing heart, shallow breathing, dizziness, nausea, flushing, and a sense of being frozen or disoriented.

The simplest, and surest, way of slowing down this panic response is to breathe. Deeply and slowly, from your stomach. Deep breathing causes the heart to slow down; it has no choice in the matter! Once your heart slows down, all the rest of the over-stimulated systems in your body will do the same.

After your horse has been spooked, his heart is usually racing. You will know he has calmed down when his breathing returns to normal. Same with us humans.

EXERCISE: MINDFUL BREATHING WITH YOUR HORSE

In this exercise we revisit the power of breathing, now in the context of what we will label "affect regulation", the ability of a person to calm down an exaggerated emotional response via somatic cues such as deep and quiet breathing. This exercise can be incorporated any time you feel that it would be beneficial to slow down the action and have the horse and client just relax together.

1. Find your center; meditate for a few minutes, focusing on your deep and quiet breathing. Check your body for any signs of stress. When you are ready, slowly approach your horse.

    With one hand on your horse's withers and one hand on his chest, gently rest your ear against the horse's neck. Begin to breath in synch with the horse. You can watch his flanks to tell when he is inhaling and exhaling. You might notice that your horse breathes much slower than you do. Try to match his rhythm.

Sharing Our Breath

2. When you are comfortable, you can try bringing your nostril down to his and breathe together, as if you are exchanging breathes. This is actually quite relaxing. Most horses are not accustomed to humans sharing nose space, so give him some time to get used to you.

How did it feel to breathe together? Connected? Serene? At peace? What would it be like to summon up this peacefulness during stressful times?

Breathing in Sync…nose to nose

3. Now notice how your horse responds when you act anxious or nervous. Anxiety is highly contagious. You might become aware that your horse is picking up your nervousness; he is breathing a bit shallower and seems more jumpy and agitated. Perhaps his head is up, ears alert, ready to run from

whatever prey has come to eat him! See what happens, in this situation, if you then begin to calm down your breathing. You might be forcing your calmness by intentionally slowing down and deepening your breath. Go ahead; he will not know you are cheating a bit.

SNAGS IN THE FEELING PROCESSING SYSTEM DUE TO TRAUMA

If you have a body, you are entitled to the full range of feelings. It comes with the package.

Annie Lamott

The emotional effects of severe trauma are serious and long-lasting. We use *psychological defenses,* the various means by which our psyche protects itself from being overwhelmed by unwanted feelings, as a way of coping in the world on a day-to-day basis. Some examples of psychological defenses used by trauma survivors are as follows.

Psychic Numbing: Sometimes, due to some horrific experience in our background, we abandon normal processing procedures. For example, perhaps you find yourself in serious danger and all your survival instincts scream "RUN!" But maybe escape is impossible because you are trapped and overpowered. Your brain might deaden your emotional response thereby allowing you to psychically survive the terrifying situation. Examples of such conditions might include having been raped, caught in a terrorist attack, or being beaten by a spouse. In all these cases, you cannot escape, all you can do is to numb your feelings and try to survive.

If a trauma was ongoing, for example if someone experienced continuous abuse as a child or ongoing victimization by a spouse, they might be conditioned to shut off feelings for as long as the abuse continues. After time, the emotional faucet might get stuck on "off." Many people remain unaware that they have stopped feeling, numbness becomes their new normal. When this happens the world loses its colors and vibrancy.

In both cases, whether a temporary or long term shutting down of feelings occurs, the psychological defense is called *Psychic Numbing*. This is similar to the process that happens when we are physically injured. After an accident, we might walk to a hospital with a broken leg, numbing ourselves to the pain. We finally allow ourselves to feel our injury *once* we have arrived somewhere safe. Both psychic and physical numbing are designed to let us survive incredible pain. However, the world rarely feels safe once you have been severely traumatized; psychic numbing becomes a way of being.

Hypo-arousal (the reverse of hyper-arousal) is another way of referring to psychic numbing. We will learn that this defensive mechanism, though effective in the immediate situation, can result in long-term emotional problems.

Horses have a highly tuned ability to remember pain and the situations and people associated with it. Put in circumstances that replicate this history, they might either become highly agitated and aggressive (hyper-arousal) or passive and withdrawn (hypo-arousal). Since they cannot speak to us, it is up to their human handlers to learn what triggers them and hopefully overcome these painful memories with kindness and consistency.

Disassociation: Another powerful psychological defense triggered by terrifying situations is call *disassociation*. If we find ourselves trapped in a terrifying situation, we might disassociate from the here and now; we stop associating to what is going on around us. We psychologically distance ourselves from the overwhelming pain and fear by blocking out what is *actually* happening to us. Some people report leaving their bodies; floating over the scene or watching from a safe distance as they are being abused. Others might focus their attention on an object, such as a tree in the backyard or a picture on the wall, successfully distracting themselves from their pain. The actual memory of the painful event and/or the feelings associated with it, remain blocked.

Dissociating from a terrifying experience might work temporarily to protect us, but the long-term tradeoff is costly. People who have relied on dissociation in the past, report not feeling present for their lives, deadened to joy, often complaining of being "spacey" and distracted. These feelings escalate during periods of stress or anxiety. To make matters worse, the unprocessed memories can come back unbidden in the form of flashbacks and nightmares.

When working with someone who becomes dissociated, they might appear vacant and distant, or the opposite, overwhelmed, shaky, perhaps childlike and panicked. In either case, the person has "left" the here and now and is now in a state of dissociation.

We can help ground someone who has dissociated by helping them to return to the present moment via mindfulness techniques. Suggest that they begin to notice what is happening *right now*. Have them describe what they see, hear, and feel, e.g. "I see the horses. I hear them nibbling their breakfast. I feel a bit cold. I can smell the hay. I am here, in the barn, on a winter morning." Remind them that they are safe; nothing that can hurt them. They are not alone. Invite them to breathe deeply, perhaps taking in the aroma of the new straw that has just been put down in the paddocks, to notice the sun coming up over the trees, to simply take in the peacefulness of the moment, this moment.

When a child is frightened, adults automatically behave in a calming, reassuring manner. "Everything is going to be O.K. You're safe." We can provide the same reassurance for someone who is flooded by frightening feelings.

Do not initiate touch with people in dissociated states. You might want to comfort them with a hug, but in this moment, they might not know who you are and it can make matters much worse.

The same defense mechanism of dissociation is experienced by horses. Your horse might be panicked by something in the environment that elicits a memory of abuse and harsh treatment. Perhaps a loud voice or seeing a whip might activate memories of cruel handling by a former owner. He might, all of a sudden, become agitated and aggressive. Again, the goal is to ground him in the here and now, reminding him that he is safe, no one will hurt him. Quiet your voice; remain calm but controlled, repeating with gentle authority, "Steady." You are here; you are in charge. Nothing can harm him.

Or your horse might respond by being quiet and remote, perhaps hanging his head, appearing tired and withdrawn. His eyes may be vacant and sad. Again, use reassuring words in a calming voice, stand quietly with him breathing deeply and slowly. If he approaches you or reaches out to you in any way, you could begin stroking his neck, just as his mother did when he was a colt. Make sure to never startle a dissociated horse; we cannot predict what he will do to protect himself. Remember, in both cases, humans and horses, they might not know who you are in that moment; they are lost to themselves and the present.

Ongoing loss of contact with one's inner self: In less traumatic situations, we might learn to mask our true feelings so well and for so long that we finally lose touch with ourselves. Many people are unaware that they have become disconnected from their feelings until someone who honestly cares asks, "How are you feeling?" and they honestly don't know. Emotions have become unavailable to them, a lost file somewhere in the system.

There are a myriad of reasons why we learn to hide our true emotions from others… and eventually ourselves. Perhaps as a child no one noticed or cared if you were hurt or scared. There was nobody who cared enough to attend to your needs; you were on your own. Or maybe there was so much stress and chaos in your family that you learned to deny your own needs while you took care of others.

As a child, your sadness and neediness might have been met with anger, impatience, and hostility. The infamous "I'll give you something to cry about!" might be a too familiar refrain. Why bother feeling? It just hurts. So you stop, you cut your feelings off. This is often referred to as "soul murder." Consequently, you have grown up being highly attuned to the needs and feelings of others but at a loss to articulate what *you* yourself are feeling or what *you* need.

Another way people learn to disconnect from their true feelings is via social pressure and conditioning. People often believe they have to present a certain "face" to the world to be accepted. This might be because they have had to pretend they were brave to ward off bullies or to be meek to avoid unwanted confrontations or angry when they really were ashamed and scared. After a while, the mask becomes the identity the person comes to believe about him or herself.

Horses help us get back in touch with our cut-off selves in a nonjudgmental, empathic manner. In the following chapters you will find exercises that will help you reawaken that part of you that has been in trance for so many years. You might have been waiting for the prince's kiss to rouse you, but horse licks, though somewhat messy, are maybe even better!

In Chapter Four we reviewed the interaction between trauma and brain functioning, particularly the limbic system and amygdala hijack. The horse, being a prey animal, is highly responsive to any threat in the environment. Horses depend on their finely tuned startle response to enable them to survive in the wild.

By calming our limbic system, via deep breathing and mindfulness, we also calm down our horse partner who is picking up our nervousness. In reverse, when we anticipate a horse being spooked, we can transmit our calmness and our sense of control to the horse who responds by quieting.

Chapter Five

Storm Tossed: In the Hurricane of Your Emotions

I am no longer afraid of storms, for I am learning how to sail my ship.

Louise May Alcott

When your feelings overwhelm you, when you are lost in the turbulent sea of your emotions, it is hard to find your way back to your true self. You are literally flooded, drowning in fear, panic, and rage. Where is your life boat - the quietness, the perspective and resiliency needed to calm the inner turmoil? How do you access the inner wisdom that this will not last forever, the storm will abate?

Dan Siegel, author of *Mindsight,* talks about a "Window of Tolerance" which is the ability to endure a surge of powerful feelings without becoming flooded. Flooding is just what it sounds like. When your car's engine becomes flooded, the whole system shuts down and the car dies. When people get emotionally flooded, they also shut down, become numb and deadened to the world, *or* they go into hyper overdrive like a child overwhelmed by anxiety.

Ideally, developing the psychic muscles needed to effectively deal with uncomfortable feelings, such as frustration and disappointment, ought to begin in infancy and continue through early childhood. By the time an individual reaches adulthood, they hopefully have acquired their own effective coping mechanisms and strategies to deal with adversity.

Those people who failed to develop emotional resiliency as children are at greater risk of being flooded. Any traumatic experience that the individual may have experienced as a child, compounds this fragility leaving them even more vulnerable to flooding.

However, even with the best of early childhood experiences, some traumatic events can be so overwhelming that the strongest individuals can be upended. For example, 9/11 touched so many people in so many damaging and powerful ways. Even if you were the most resilient person in the world with the best coping skills, this catastrophe would shake you, profoundly.

Bring in the horses! How can we use our partnership with horses to help strengthen and expand our Window of Tolerance? What can we learn from these peaceful creatures that live totally in the moment, who feel their feeling (be it fear, hunger, terror) and then quickly return to their normal state of quietude?

Dan Siegel, in *Mindsight*, talks of the power of R.A.I.N., an acronym for a useful sequence of techniques to employ when faced with a potentially traumatic experience:

R. RECOGNIZE what is happening in *this* moment. Label the feeling. "I am angry." "I am terrified." "I am sad." No judgment, just a noticing.

A. ACCEPT that this is what is, with awareness and compassion. This is what I am feeling as this moment.

I. INVESTIGATE the feeling, exploring its dimensions, size, color, beliefs that sustain it.

N. NON-IDENTIFY that "I am more than this wave of emotions." "I am more than the events that have happened to me."

For example, perhaps you have been in a fender bender on the highway. You might *recognize* that you are feeling upset. You could *accept* that this is what is, someone hit your car, and of course you are going to feel distressed. You *realize* that you tend to blame yourself for any misfortune and though you want to make it about you, you choose not to. You *accept* that there was nothing you could have done. It happened. Even if it was your fault, people are fallible. We have accidents. That is what insurance is for. You *investigate* your automatic feelings and work to not allow that black cloud of shame to descend on you. You *gain perspective* on the event. I had an accident. You non-identify. That does not make me a horrible, careless person. I know myself to be a responsible driver. I won't allow this incident to color my confidence in driving.

As wonderful as Dan Seigel's model is, it is cognitively based. As we have discussed, so much of what happens to us during crisis is processed in a non-verbal, limbic-driven manner. The incoming information rarely makes it to the prefrontal cortex for processing.

EXERCISE: FIELD WORK –OBSERVING THE HERD IN A NATURALISTIC SETTING

This exercise helps the client to notice how horses can get unsettled, spooked, agitated, annoyed, and then quickly returned to grazing, chomping away at the grass as if the brouhaha never happened. This is also a great exercise for the beginning EEP client or group to spend time observing horses in action.

Anthropologists embed themselves in tribes, a la Margaret Mead and the Samoans. They quietly observe the habits, customs, and rituals of the people that they are studying. Pretend you are a horse anthropologist. Join a herd of horses for a few hours, just be there and notice. Watch the interplay between the horses, the power plays between the dominant and submissive horses. You can nudge this along by bringing a carrot or two and watch how one horse will push, nudge, and even snap at other contenders to make sure they know their place in carrot hierarchy handout time.

Make sure you have a horse person with you who knows the herd, since this could get nasty if one horse is particularly grabby and grouchy. Horses are usually put outside with their buddies, but even buddies can get annoying at times! You will surely see a lot of "Who moves whom?" playing out, as the horses vie for dominance.

Notice that during a horsey spat or a bit of a scare (a runaway turkey waddles across their path or a low flying plane vibrates the ground and makes a huge noise) the horses become agitated, alert, on edge. Watch how quickly after the perceived danger is over, they are able to return to their normal, placid grazing. Their breathing slows down, their heads drop from high and alert to hanging somewhat low, their ears come forward from having been flattened on their heads. "I wasn't killed. That's good. Let's go eat."

If you watch nature shows (for those of you who don't get upset by watching animals eating other animals….not everyone's cup of tea!) or have been on safaris, you notice that after a major scare, after a herd of whatevers are being chased by whomevers, the prey animals return to their normal grazing behavior. Their systems quickly calm down, and life goes on.

We humans, however, often get stuck in terror. The fear, imagined or real, overwhelms our tolerance level, and we stop processing information in a linear fashion. We don't get to experience the terrifying incident, integrate it, and move on as other animals seem to. We have the wonderful ability, because of our higher cognitive processing, to dwell, ruminate, and worry ourselves silly, about whatever event scared us silly. Sometimes progress is a mixed blessing!

How do horses integrate terrorizing events and seamlessly return to normal? Let us look at the effect of being grounded in our reality so that random scary events fail to uproot us. Maybe we can learn this Zen-like skill from our equine therapists.[10]

GROUNDING YOURSELF DURING TURBULENT TIMES

Rootlessness is the discomforting experience of being disconnected from and afloat in the universe with nothing anchoring you. You are at the mercy of the elements, in this case, your own internal storms. But how do we go about growing roots?

The childhood experience of being anchored in our family of origin is the first step in developing a sense of connection with others. We are not alone; we are part of something greater than ourselves. Unfortunately, many of us were brought up in families that were too chaotic, or too precarious for any meaningful connection and grounding to occur. Our families were not our cove in the storm, but the storm itself.

Others of us have had our roots torn away by the explosive power of traumatizing events, for example surviving a terrorist attack or being the victim of a violent crime. Our connection to ourselves and to humanity has been radically severed.

With the help of our horse co-therapists, we can begin to discover how to ground ourselves so that we become more resilient to life's unexpected storms and upheavals.

We have found that lunging a horse is a wonderful way to help people: a) rehearse staying centered and grounded, b) practice maintaining a connection to the horse, c) enhance mastery and self-efficacy, and d) allow for the wonderfully childish fantasy of being part of a circus!

Lunging is basically having your horse circle around you either on a lunge line or at liberty. Usually, lunging is used to exercise a horse and to have them practice their various gaits. In EEP, we use lunging to deepen the connection between

---

[10] For further information on this phenomenon, please see: Levine, Peter, A. *Waking The Tiger – Healing Trauma.*

the horse and client as well as practicing mindfulness, maintaining attention and concentration, and mastering a sense of self-efficacy.

EXERCISE: BEGINNING LUNGING

We will use lunging for a number of exercise. Lunging requires being able to maintain a quiet state of mindfulness and connectivity and can be used in any situation that requires the above skills. Lunging should be incorporated only when the client has become comfortable with horses.

Lunging requires total connection with the horse. If you dis-connect for any reason, the horse will come to a quiet stop, almost as if you took your foot off the gas pedal in the car. You need to remain mindful and in the moment when you are lunging a horse.

Major Warning! Make sure the lunge line is not circling your hand but folded so that, if necessary, you can let go. The first time I tried lunging Bixby, upon transitioning to a canter, he decided it was the perfect moment to take off toward the yummy grass on the opposite side of the huge paddock. And, boy, am I glad my hand did not go with him!

1. Ready? You are in the center of an imaginary circle connected to your horse via a lunge line (very long lead line). Send your horse to the outer edge of the circle by pointing your crop at his shoulder and visualizing where you would like him to be. Picture that your crop is now a magical wand that wondrously transmits energy from you to the horse.

   Your goal is to maintain some tension in the lunge line. This provides ongoing communication with the horse, just as reins do when riding. If the line is too taut the horse is nervous and pulling away from you. If the line is very loose, the horse is too close, you should request he move further out by pointing the wand at his shoulder.

If your horse slows down and stops or if he isn't paying attention to your cues, it means you have lost your connection to him. Take a deep breathe, ground yourself and try again. Horses are patient, forgiving creatures.

2. Point your crop at the horse's rear to get him to move forward and front of him to ask him to stop or slow down. When the horse is in movement, keep the crop pointed to where your legs would connect to his body if you were riding him. The horse expert will help you with this.

3. When you are feeling comfortable at the walk, you can ask him for a faster gait. Strengthen your voice, raising it higher at the end, at the same time as sending the energy to his rear, by directing your crop in that direction (without touching him). This will drive him forward. If you are feeling gutsy, go ahead and ask him for a canter by waving the wand forcefully at his rear. You might want to ground yourself before he really starts to fly!

   The first time I had Bixby canter on a lunge line, I was totally unprepared and off balance. That's a lot of horse energy that I was holding on to! It felt like grasping onto a kite on a wildly windy day. After my first off kilter attempt, I prepared myself by grounding and centering before I requested a canter. It also helped to give him a bit more rope to help him stay balanced *and* protect your back!

4. To get him to change direction, using your crop as a guide, send the energy around his body leading him into a turn. It helps to visualize him turning. Remember, it is hypothesized that horses think in pictures so why not join them.

5. If you are feeling brave and confident, you can try lunging your horse off the lead line. Be prepared not to take the result too seriously since this can be quite a humbling experience. Trying something difficult is wonderful for the soul and laughter is a healing balm for bruised egos.

At this point, you might be feeling a tad dizzy from turning in circles! All normal, if not humiliating, steps in the learning process. It is hard to be mindful of your horse, your breathing, your feet, the rope, etc. and do it all gracefully!

6. When you feel complete, or you and your horse look a bit lopsided, stop and breathe. Center yourself and quietly invite your horse, with open heart, to come forward for a rewarding hug or forehead nuzzle.

It takes a lot of psychic energy to maintain mindfulness, to stay in the here and now. It gets easier, promise. This is a good time for a tea and biscuit break, and you can have a carrot.

**The Magic Wand …where you point your crop
sends the energy out to the horse**

And away we go!

All lunging exercises will be performed accompanied by a horse specialist.

EXERCISE: THE TREE ARCHETYPE (LUNGING)

*Stacey Carter: Heart Centered Horsemanship

This exercise uses the symbol of trees as being timeless, grounded, and impervious to the storms and turbulence of the world around them. Taking on the attributes of an ancient tree enables our clients to experience being anchored, resilient, and centered.

Over the centuries, the tree has come to symbolize strength, groundedness, and timelessness. We talk of having "deep roots" in our family, our community, our religion. We refer to lost souls as "rootless." When we think of trees, we imagine not only their power to shelter us from storms but also their ability to survive the most violent tempests. We borrow the archetype of the tree to model the anchoring and resiliency needed to survive the upheavals of life.

1. Close your eyes and gently breathe. Stand very tall, head up, shoulders back. Now visualize your feet growing roots stretching deep into the ground. Imagine your roots growing stronger, thicker, weaving together, and creating a solid foundation anchoring you.

2. Reach your arms up. Visualize branches growing from your arms, upward to the sky, getting denser, more leaf covered, more lush.

3. Visualize your torso expanding into a thick, solid tree trunk.

4. Experience yourself as an ancient, timeless tree that has weathered the millennia.

5. Now, imagine a huge, powerful wind billowing across the field towards you. See your branches swaying with that wind, your trunk gently bending, your sturdy roots holding you securely, knowing that *this* wind, *this* passing storm, *this* moment of torment, will pass and that you will endure as you have for centuries.

6. Open your eyes, slowly. Be mindful of where you are, who you are, how you are feeling.

7. Now, lead your horse into the round pen and begin lunging him. When you are comfortable with his pace and your connection, start imagining your tree

self. Use each breath to ground you even deeper into the earth all the while maintaining your connection to the horse.

8. When you are ready, gently let go of any tension/energy you are exerting on the lead line. Relax your grasp. The horse will slow to a stop. Open your arms and heart and invite the horse to approach you. Horses tend to soften when they are protected by trees. Give him a hug, stroke, whatever feels right at that moment, welcoming him. Send him back out with your wand (crop) to once again begin lunging.

9. If you're feeling brave, go ahead and try this exercise without the lunge line; with the horse at liberty. I promise, when you get the hang of this, it feels like magic!

Notice the difference between pulling the horse to you and inviting the horse to approach you by grounding yourself. If you pull, you can easily lose your footing; through grounding, you can hold onto practically any horse.

Lunging at liberty… The Tree Archetype

Reconvene in your group. What difference would it make in your life to be grounded, to be able to exert less effort to establish the connectedness you long for? How often have you tried to "pull" someone to you, force something to happen, and in doing so lose your footing? How effective was that? Can you trust that just being grounded, by being you, people will want to approach you? Accept you?

EXERCISE: STAND YOUR GROUND – TREE EXERCISE #2

This exercise flows from the first tree exercise. It deepens the sense of being grounded and can easily be used in any situation requiring boundary maintenance, resiliency, and interpersonal challenges. Of course, the client must be comfortable with horses; this is not appropriate for beginner EEP clients.

Using the same grounding principle, we enter the game of "Who Pushes Who" that horses love to play. If you allow yourself to get pushed around, you lose, and the pusher gets to move up the herd hierarchy.

1. Head into the field with the horses. Go ahead and mingle with the herd. Eventually, someone is going to nudge you, try to get you to move, particularly if you are too close to their best friend or the pile of hay. Just hold your own, don't let yourself be pushed. I know, unfair advantage, they are way bigger than you. Grow your roots, thicken your trunk, and stand your ground! You do not have to push back. He probably would be unimpressed with that anyway. Just gather your energy and be. Notice what happens.

How did it feel to refuse to be pushed around? To be respected, not criticized, for taking care of yourself? In what areas of life would this ability to just Stand Your Ground be useful?

In Chapter Six we covered the psychic challenge of staying centered during turbulent emotional times. Dan Siegel's R.A.I.N. program was discussed as a cognitive technique used to assist someone in reappraising a potentially disturbing event. In contrast, we demonstrated how lunging a horse, on and off lead, is an effective, non-verbal way to practice staying centered.

The storm has passed and we can now continue on our journey towards self-compassion. Perhaps you and your horse would like a few minutes to just do nothing, relax. Go ahead, treat yourselves.

Chapter Six

The Art of Compassion and Self-Forgiveness

If your compassion does not include yourself, it is incomplete.

Jack Kornfield

Humans are the only species that suffer from self-loathing...thanks to our ability to self-reflect and obsess on all the mistakes we have made, people we have failed, and goals we have not attained. We are intolerant of our humanness, unable to accept anything less than perfection in everything we attempt....or not attempting it at all for fear of failure. We subject ourselves to ourselves on a daily basis. A puppy might feel a moment of humiliation if it ate your sock. Or a horse might feel somewhat abashed if it accidently hurt something littler than itself. However, those feelings are just a moment's fleeting response to having love and approval withdrawn. How quickly the puppy returns to its "I am a wonderful thing!" stance once you have petted it on the head and love is restored. And the horse goes about munching its hay, not dwelling on the fact that it just squashed your toes. We humans do a fabulous job of holding onto, nurturing, embellishing, and clinging to our self-criticism. It is very difficult, nay impossible, to appreciate your life when you are busy hating yourself.

Look at a horse in the field, contentedly grazing. Does he look like he is dwelling on Woody Allenish neurotic worries? Has he had a tough childhood? Very likely, yes. Many people treat horses as objects that exist for the owner's pleasure. But he doesn't appear to be dwelling on it.

When a new horse arrives at Becky's stable, he is assessed to see if he might need help adjusting, learning to trust, and/or being touched and approached. He cannot tell you, and his previous owners most probably are not going to own up to any past abuse or mistreatment. Thankfully, most horses are not mistreated, but many, in the name of "training," are "broken" and their spirits extinguished.

Most horses heal quickly from emotional trauma if treated with kindness, consistency, and clear communication. It does not take them long to realize that they are in a safe place. No one is going to hurt them or mistreat them here. They learn this by interacting and relating to caring people and socializing with calm, accepting horses. Like most emotionally wounded creatures, safety, time, and trust are the keys to recovery.

Bixby, one of my favorite riding buddies, obviously had some troubling experiences in his previous stable. When he came to us, he was very wary of the other horses, angrily protective of his food, and skittish with both the humans and horses. His ears would automatically go back when anyone approached him in his stall. He would snap at you if you came too close during feed time and would hover protectively around his food bucket even if it was empty. But he loved going out on trail. So off we went and had a number of relaxing walks together where Bixby was present, confident, and involved in everything we passed. He was responsive to my aids and let me pet him on his neck as we trotted along. It took a while, but now Bixby is a happy, contented horse with a new best equine friend. He is much more approachable and calm and will actually go over to say hello to you… and see if you have brought him munchies. He still will get a bit peevish if you come too close during his feed time, but in general he is a much more trusting, sweet horse.

EXERCISE: PRACTICING COMPASSION

In this exercise we employ the psychological mechanism known as projection (when someone projects onto another something about themselves) to help our clients identify their often disparaging and judgmental self-assessments. Empathy and appreciation for the horse's struggle, and by association their own, helps rewrite their self-critical script. This is a form of Cognitive Reframing, part of a Cognitive Behavioral approach to healing.

1. Gather in a group. Breathe and center. In your notebook, write down a list of all the endeavors you feel you have miserably failed at, the goals you have not reached nor even started, the multitude of ways you have disappointed everyone in your life, including yourself. Go ahead and be as self-critical as you can. Seep yourself in guilt and self-loathing. No one will see this list; no one will judge you except you, your harshest critique.

2. A horse that had some serious behavioral issues resulting from past abusive experiences will be introduced to the group. (Therapists, feel free to be creative here. The horse won't mind if you exaggerate his past misery; he knows it is for a good purpose.) We will discuss his history up until the time he arrived at the stable.

3. Next, as if he were a good, dear friend, you are to list all the wonderful things about him, for example, the resiliency he demonstrated by coming this far in his emotional recovery. Perhaps he has been able to risk having someone lunge him or has befriended a shy horse. Each of you will have the opportunity to express your compassion and caring to the horse.

4. Return to your notebook and write down some wonderful things about yourself including the courage and determination it took for you to come this far in your life including coming to the barn today. How many obstacles have you had to overcome? Divorce? Abuse? Addiction?

Abandonment/Neglect? Serious career issues? Illness? Have you ever stopped to acknowledge and appreciate what it took to overcome these challenges?

Notice, with compassion, how incredibly tough you are on yourself yet how gentle and encouraging you can be towards others.

5. Each of you will get an opportunity, if you so wish, to read this list back to the group. Here is an opportunity to acknowledge how your life experiences have taught you about compassion, for yourself and others. The group can add to the list the valuable things they have learned about you.

HEALING FROM SHAME

Countless times I have seen fear turn to acceptance of self…a person closed to intimacy turn to a horse when they were unable or unwilling to turn to people."

Don Lavendar

Sadly, many adults who have had difficult childhoods or survived a trauma are often left feeling shamed and "different" from other people because of their experiences. They might describe themselves as "toxic" or "alien" or "contaminated." Regardless of the fact that they were often *the victims* of an event, shame and guilt seem to coexist with the experience of trauma.

Shame is the feeling that there is something inherently wrong with you, something repellent to others. For example, if your parents constantly told you that you were bad instead of "What you did was bad," you might grow up believing that about yourself. Or, perhaps if you were molested as a child, you might feel as if you carried a shameful secret, that you are toxic and dirty and somehow blameworthy. Perhaps you stayed in an abusive relationship and you feel as if people judge you harshly for not having left earlier. Or perhaps, upon returning from active duty, you feel you cannot let go of the fact that you survived while your buddies didn't. You are not the same person you were when you left for war; you can no longer live up to people's expectations. You withhold sharing your feelings in fear of being judged or misunderstood and risk further alienation. Your isolation is unbearable.

Shame is like the mold you find in your basement. Mold flourishes in dark, isolated places. If you want to get rid of mold, say on your favorite cowboy boots or winter coat, you expose it to the sun. The same with shame. If you want to lower or eliminate shame, share it...put it in the sun. It cannot survive once it is exposed. Shame is the "secret" emotion which takes on power by virtue of its covert nature.

This is the significant difference between privacy and secrecy. Privacy is a healthy boundary created around personal information that you might or might not share depending on circumstances and people. For example, you might not share how much your income is with people you are not close to; it is none of their business.

Secrecy, unlike privacy, is usually about something shameful, something that you do not want others to know about you. For example, if you were incested as a child, the powerful message that the abuser conveys to you, either verbally or covertly, is that this is a secret....a toxically powerful secret. If you shared what happened to you, it would cause irreparable harm to you and your family. It becomes your responsibility to hold this secret, a weighty burden for a child. Or, your very powerful, respected husband is physically abusive. The thought of going for help is anathema. It would destroy the family, your husband, your economic standing, and who would believe you anyway? So you hold the shameful secret, a lonely burden you must carry.

It is hard to be truly intimate with others if you feel as if you have to hide "the ugly" part of yourself. Working with our horse co-therapist, we can work on healing shame, secrecy, and the isolation it imposes on us.

EXERCISE: SHINING LIGHT ON SHAME

This exercise can be used throughout a session, whenever you feel that the client could use some alone time with the horse.

A client who has been unable to share a shameful part of their past might be willing to risk sharing it with a horse. The toxic secret they have been forced to carry for so many lonely years is now a shared experience…and nothing bad happened. Actually saying what is forbidden out loud is deeply healing.

- First practice deep breathing on your own and then synchronize your breathing with your horse.
- Quietly tell him something about yourself that you have not risked sharing with others, perhaps in fear of judgment, shame, or rejection.
- Lean on him, let him carry the weight of your secrets. He can handle the burden. Stay as close to him for as long as you need.

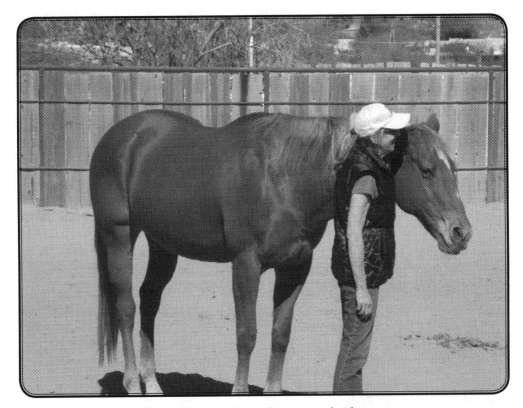

Sharing My Burdens and Shame

How does this feel? Could you imagine confiding this toxic secret to someone you trust? Can you imagine someone sharing with you something that they feel shameful about? How would you respond? Don't you deserve the same compassion that you would give to others?

SELF-FORGIVENESS

I once was lost, but now am found. Was blind but now can see.
Amazing Grace

Many of us, particularly those wounded in childhood, wander the earth feeling like a burden to others, believing that our needs are too big, our guilt too large, and our shame too overwhelming to risk sharing our true selves. Who would want such an encumbrance?

You might not be aware of holding yourself and your dreams back. You might not even be aware of exactly what you want and hope for, having survived by exquisitely tuning into the wants and needs of others.

To begin to learn what you deserve as a human being, and then to finally risk asking for it, takes a tremendous amount of courage. What would it be like to allow yourself to lean on another when life becomes just too hard and your problems too heavy to carry by yourself?

Horses have large hearts and powerful bodies. They are nonjudgmental and, by nature, nurturing. They can bear the weight of your needs, including the need to just rest on them for a while.

EXERCISE: LAY MY BURDEN DOWN

This exercise can be used throughout a session when you feel as if your client needs to "rest" with the horse; to let go or share something that has been weighing on them. This is very similar to Shining Light On Shame but adds a different level of trust to the encounter. Can something or somebody actually share the burden of my life with me? Can I stop feeling so alone in the world?

1. Become centered: enter your body via deep breathing and mindfulness.

2. Walk up to the horse, and as you did with co-breathing, put one arm across his chest and one arm along his body.

3. Tell the horse, privately, what you need to share, let go of, need help with. Perhaps you would like to whisper to him something you have been too ashamed to reveal to others. He is listening. He will not judge.

4. Now, with your face resting on his strong neck and your arm securely around his chest, let your whole body, all your weight, be supported by the horse. You will not overwhelm him; your weight will not disturb him. Rest there. Breathe quietly. Lean on him for as long as you like.

5. When you feel complete, step back and thank the horse…in whatever way feels real for you…could be a pat, a nuzzle, an eye to eye check in.

I Can Rest On You, There Is No Judgement.

How do you feel? Where do you feel it? What part of your experience would you like to bring into your world with you? What difference would it make in your life if you could risk asking others to share your burdens?

Alita H. Buzel

EXERCISE: SHARING THE WEIGHT

This exercise is another technique for allowing others to share our problems, but in a more metaphorical way.

1. You'll be given a saddlebag filled with heavy rocks. While holding onto the bag, your challenge is to halter your horse with your one free hand. When you are able to successfully halter the horse or decide it is not worth the frustration, step back.
2. This time, attach the saddlebag onto the pummel on the saddle. *Now* put the halter on the horse. Easier without having to carry the extra burden!
3. Discuss what "burdens" you might be dragging around with you. They could be toxic secrets, guilt, an overly dependent friend, a hidden addiction or compulsion. The list is endless.

Discuss how it felt to give the burden over to the horse. Did the horse seem resentful or annoyed at having to carry your burden? How hard was it to "ask" for help? Could you imagine sharing your burden with someone dear to you, someone you trust? How might that feel?

In Chapter Six we explored compassion for self and others, and noticed how we are our own worst critics. As Woody Allen said in "Annie Hall" "… I don't want to be a part of a group that would have me as a member"

The nature of shame as a universal experience was discussed along with the healing power of sharing. We began to understand and appreciate the isolation inherent in carrying around a toxic secret. Again, with the help of our therapy horse, we practiced the art of nonjudgmental self-love and forgiveness and the courage to truly lean on another.

Time for fun!

Chapter Seven

Developing Resiliency and Rediscovering Joy

The most beautiful people we have known are those who have known defeat, known struggle, known loss, and have found their way out up from the depths.

Annie Lamott

In life, it is not our personal history or what challenges we have faced that determine our ability to survive and thrive. Instead, it is the capacity to negotiate with reality, to find creative ways around obstacles, to reframe our failures into life lessons that makes the difference between happiness and contentment or bitterness and defeat.

SETTING GOALS AND STICKING TO THEM!

Anyone who has worked with a horse knows that what *you* plan to do and what will actually happen is often quite a different animal! Setting a goal, whether it is walking your brave steed past that very frightening paper bag flapping in the wind or approaching your boss for a raise – takes clarity, determination, stick-to-it-ness and a bit of bravery. It also means being flexible. If one approach fails to work, how about trying a different one instead of giving up in defeat? The ability to keep going in spite of your fears and failures is called resilience. Resilience is a powerful determinant in getting what you want out of life, regardless of what hurdles are thrown in your way.

Using your horse therapist, let's attempt some resiliency drills.

EXERCISE: LEADING 101:

The following set of exercises focus on setting life goals (in these case, horse goals) and learning to negotiate the inevitable bumps and obstacles that characterize all journeys. The ability to be self-forgiving, to face each challenge in an open and curious manner, to be able to laugh at yourself when everything goes kaput, to stumble, get back up and keep going, are all essential life skills. When these exercises are done in groups, your clients get to practice sharing responsibility and being supportive and encouraging of each other. What is important is the journey, not winning or losing. Isn't that what life should be about?

Leading a horse where you want it to go sounds like an easy task; however the degree of success of your horsey venture depends on the horse, its mood, the weather, your energy, the gods…. Remember, this exercise is about *resiliency*. Keep trying, change techniques, and, when all else fails, laugh at and with yourself. We cannot chose what happens on our journey, but we can choose to enjoy the ride.

Part I: Meandering with your horse

l. First, breathe and center. Visualize what you want to happen…in this case, taking a pleasant and leisurely stroll with your horse across the paddock. Usually, horses are trying to figure out what we want and are anxious to please us. Notice, I said "usually!"

2. *With full intention,* step off confidently, your lead rope in your right hand hanging slack between you and your horse (remembering not to loop it around your hand). *Expect* the horse to follow you. Now, the horse will decide whether to make life easy for you or make you work!

Actually, horses are not that manipulative. If they appear not to listen to you, you probably aren't asking clearly for what you want. You are allowed to ask for help from the horse specialist. No one expects you to master Horse Talk. Here is a great opportunity to *Not Take It Personally* or project all sorts of nasty attributes on your "stubborn" horse!

3. Once you and your horse start to go, *do not look back at him*. You know what he looks like. Instead, focus your attention on where *you* want to go…perhaps the other side of the pen, the oak tree in the back, wherever your heart desires. Visual it. Just work on keeping that goal clearly in your mind.

4. If your horse hangs back, and you will know this when you are moving forward without a horse and with a taut rope, try raising the intensity of your request by tightening your right hand on the lead, producing a pressure that will travel up the rope to the halter. The minute you sense the horse is even *thinking* about moving, release your grip. We ALL prefer working without pressure even though we might need a little to get ourselves going.

5. If that does not get him moving, try a little slap with the end of your lead on his rump. That should work. It will not hurt him! Promise.

6. Remember to give the guy some time when you request anything. He might appear to be just standing there, but he is probably waiting for a bit more guidance from you.

Part II: Picking up the pace

1. Once you have your horse going on the lead, gradually increase the length of your stride for a few paces. IF your horse picks up his pace to match yours, stop for a moment, turn, breathe, and give a hug, or handshake if that feels more comfortable.

2. After a short pause, lead off again at a slow pace. In three or four paces, pick up the speed of your stride even faster, so that your horse has to hustle to keep up. Remember to always keep the horse nearer the gate…no need to accidently get squashed.

3. If you are feeling adventurous, or do not mind feeling humiliated if the horse takes off in the opposite direction, try the above two steps without a lead.

Being Wonderfully In Sync

FACTORING IN FEAR, PROCRASTINATION, PERFECTIONISM AND AVOIDANCE

When you make friends with fear, it can't rule you.

Anne Lamott

Before we can begin to work towards any goal, we first have to START! Starting is a *big* problem for a lot of human beings and they have an array of interesting, clever, and argue-proof reasons to not even begin a venture. This "starting" problem falls under the all-purpose label of procrastination. You are putting the emotional gas on, you *want* to get going, but nothing happens. You've flooded your engine with fear.

A favorite excuse that I often here is, "I must be lazy." Usually the people who use this justification are *anything but* lazy. They squash in a million tasks a day, juggle impressive amounts of responsibilities, yet truly believe they're lazy. Right. How about, "I'm scared." "I'm anxious." "If I don't do it perfectly, I'm an abject failure." "If I never try, I'll never find out I'm an abject failure and I can hold onto the image of myself as a: writer, actor, go getter, champion equestrian, loveable person." I never said this made sense. I just said we're all human. You'd never see a horse procrastinate. That would just be silly. I agree.

So before beginning any exercise, I would invite your clients to acknowledge their feelings about even trying. Noted, it is a little easier to go along with the crowd during an equine therapy session, then overcoming their fear and hesitation when facing a challenge alone.

GROUP EXERCISE: HORSE OLYMPICS: EVENT ONE

Laughter is the shortest distance between two people.

Victor Borge

There is no perfect way to do this exercise, no right or wrong. The aim is to stay in the moment and enjoy the pure fun and playfulness of the game. Half the joy of the journey is getting there, however lopsided the "journey" becomes.

As a group, be clear about your goal, e.g. to lead your buddy around the round pen or perhaps to lead him through an obstacle course of your personal design. The horse will be off his lead, so he has a vote in what he chooses to do.

1. Agree upon the role each member is to take. One person on left of the horse, one on right (or two depending on our number), and one person in front to

"draw" the horse forward, forming a human triangle. Front positions set the pace.

2. Once the group trusts that the horse has agreed to play with you, off you go…hopefully with the horse. Remember, a horse's favorite game is to see who moves whom, so if he starts to push into your territory, do not hesitate to push him back. Quick reminder: watch his feet. Trust yourself, trust the horse, and focus on your intention! Your group gets extra points for laughing.

3. When your group feels complete (does not mean reaching the original goal), time for a group hug! (Include the horse, please). Everyone gets a carrot.

EXERCISE: HORSE OLYMPICS: EVENT TWO

1. Your team lines up between two buckets filled with water. The people at each end of the line must hold the buckets. You cannot break the line though it can take any shape you would like, half circle, straight, up to you. Hand holding is allowed!

2. *Without touching the horse*, your team has to move the horse to the opposite side of the round pen. Remember, you have to stay in your line! There are a lot of obstacles and choices here, as in life! Be creative, be resilient, and have fun! Each team will have about five minutes to achieve their goal.

After each game, review with your team. How hard was it to find alternative ways to get the horse to do what you requested (or hoped for!)? Did you notice yourself getting self-critical? Blaming the horse? Your team mates? When did you give up being frustrated and taking this personally and just give in to laughter? What was this experience like for you? How do you think the horse feels right about now?

The Zen Of Horse

Think about what it would be like to appreciate the journey without being so focused on the outcome? The Eastern philosophy of reincarnation is wonderfully non-focused on goals. Since time is circular, why hurry or fret? You will be back at the same place where you started anyway! Our western sense of time is linear.... always heading somewhere, the sooner we get "there" the better. Just being with horses and playing with them, gives us the opportunity to relax and enjoy the ride. And sometimes that *is* the goal!

HORSING AROUND – RECLAIMING OUR INALEINABLE RIGHT TO JOY

Your body cannot heal without play. Your mind cannot heal without laughter. Your soul cannot heal without joy.

Catherine Ripened Fenwick

So many of us have lost our laughter. We have lost our ability to play, to be silly and spontaneous. I have seen numerous pictures of my patients as happy, little kids or carefree young adults. That was before....before whatever befell them darkened their lives rendering them but a shadow of their former, joyous selves. When we rediscover our laughter, we also rediscover the self-forgiveness, innocence, and compassion that were stolen from us so long ago.

When the Dalai Lama was asked his philosophy regarding self-criticism, he looked confused. "What is self-criticism?" he inquired. When it was explained he was astounded, "Why would anyone do such a thing?" Why indeed?

Being in the company of a horse is serious business. You need to be attentive and aware at all moments of what is going on - with the horse, with yourself, and with the horse and you. You should remain on quiet alert, ready to steady your horse when a deer jumps across your path or stray dogs come barking. But you can be having a great time at the same time; and you should be! Life constantly flows between the serious and the playful.

This is great! I'm out in the woods on a gorgeous fall day. I'm laughing with my friends and singing to my horse. My horse (let's call him Bixby) is enjoying looking around, being out and about, bumping into his friend as we pass on the trail. Perhaps a bit of horseplay? (Not when I'm on your back, you don't!)

If you cannot find something funny or sweet or amusing on your outing with your horse buddy, if you do not find yourself smiling, humming, singing cowboy songs to your horse (my specialty), then you are missing out on joy. And it is so there for the asking.

How do we go about reclaiming childlike wonder and fun? How can we remember, when we are with our horse wandering through the woods, that this is not a test! No one is judging us or even looking at us. We are not performing; we are just being. As long as you do not yank the poor guy's neck too hard or confuse the hell out of him about what you want him to do, he is ready to have fun with you. (He loves being out on a trail! There are so many interesting smells and objects.) You have worked hard all week. You have been under incredible pressure. You have pushed yourself to your limits and beyond. How do you turn all that off when you are on a horse, bopping along a country trail, on a beautiful, clear, brisk autumn day?

Remember how safe you are. Right this moment. One of the requirements of play is to feel safe. What could make you feel a bit safer *right now*? Something you could remind yourself of? Noticing your friends around you on their horses? Noticing how calm and content your horse is? Reminding yourself that the last person out on trail on your horse was an eight year old…and she made it back alive!

Next time you head out on trail or start a lesson, why not practice your mindfulness. There will be so many smells, feelings, sensations, noises, and colors, to be noticed. Imagine not criticizing yourself or chronically judging your riding skills harshly. Imagine leaving all your worries outside the barn; they will be waiting for you when it is time for you to leave. So you do not have to worry about worrying.

GROUP EXERCISE: HORSEY SOCCER

This game requires that you divide into two teams. A prize will be given for the team with the most horse-appropriate/and or silliest name. Goal lines will be marked off at either side of the paddock which will be divided in half. One team will start on the right, the other on the left. We do not need head-on collisions!

The goal is to get your horse to cross over your goal line. The horse will be free to follow you or not. You cannot touch the horse or bribe him with carrots. You job is to encourage him to move with the team. Whichever team gets its horse to the goal line first wins! I have no clue what you win, but if you are not laughing by the time this is over, I will be a horse's uncle! Make sure your human team is in the front and sides of your horse, not in back of him. No tailgating allowed!

If there are enough of you, you can split your team up like a relay race with one part of the team waiting at the goal line to take over and lead the horse home. Cheering is allowed, but no sudden movements or flag waving please!

*With this game, each team will also have a horse specialist who will act as the coach and keep everything fair and safe.

Review with your group.

- What was it like to play this game? Did it bring up any familiar issues?
- Did you feel you were part of the team, or did you have a bit of an issue with joining in?
- What was it like for you to take part in something totally silly and playful?
- Were you able to let go and not worry how you were being judged by others?
- What do you think this game was like for the horse?

How could you incorporate playfulness into your life? Could you freeze frame in your memory a carefree moment that caught you laughing? What part of you would you like to take home with you today? Feel free! Consider it a gift of appreciation from your horse.

Life's Journey

I'm neither bad, nor strange, just slightly rearranged
Mary Chapin Carpenter

As we go through our life's journey, there are many points in time…poignant events, transitions, tragedies… that leave us forever changed. No one gets away with leading a pain-free, uneventful life and how boring if we did! We have all experienced being lost, out of control, hurt, betrayed, and frightened.

The challenge is to integrate these experiences into a cohesive narrative, a hard earned wisdom. All things happen for a reason; all will make sense, perhaps not in the moment but in the long term.

GROUP EXERCISE: BUMPY JOURNEY "You've Gotta Crack a Few Eggs" *Tracie Faa-Thompson: "Harnessing the Power of Equine Assisted Counseling"*

I'm all the ages I've ever been.
Annie Lamott

This exercise incorporates playfulness, interpersonal cooperation, dealing with frustrating circumstances, and reframing life histories. Since a significant part of this experience is sharing painful events, it should be done only with groups that have been working together for a while and share the level of trust necessary for this level of personal revelation.

1. Take a human buddy into the ring where your trusty steed will be waiting. Write on the first page of your notebook: "The Beginning of My Story." That

"Beginning" could be your birth, your first memory, or whatever you choose to designate as the beginning of You.

2. You will be given a hardboiled egg. Place the egg wherever you want on the horse. You can hold it in place until you and the horse begins to move.

3. Now, start walking with your horse…and egg. Your goal is to get from one side of the paddock to the other. You can try to catch the egg when it falls. Do not worry; we expect the egg to drop many times on its journey from "The Beginning" to the "Here and Now."

4. Each time the egg falls, have your human buddy write in your notebook a significant event that has happened to you as you traveled through your life. Put the egg back on the horse and keep going. Laughing is definitely allowed and encouraged. No one can do this exercise and look graceful! Life is full of funny and fun moments to be cherished, even in the midst of recalling pain. Think how often horses would laugh if they could (particularly at us!).

5. After all of you have had a chance to take your journey, re-group. Each person has an opportunity to describe their now badly cracked egg. Any thoughts, feelings, and/or insights are welcome during this sharing session. Of course, you only share what you feel comfortable with.

6. Take some time to look at what is written in your notebook. How have you integrated and made meaning of these events in your life story? How have these experiences changed you, for better or for worse? What were you meant to learn from them? What experiences still need to be integrated, are too new, or too painful to look at via the wisdom of hindsight. Put those away, they will make sense to you with time.

7. As you look at your cracked egg, how do you feel? You might notice how all the cracks give the egg character, etching history onto the original blank white canvas. You might appreciate how the shell protected the more vulnerable, soft inside from being hurt. Give yourself a hug; give someone else a hug. Save one for the horse.

EXERCISE – JUST BEING

This exercise is a wonderfully simple opportunity for the client to just be with their therapy horse. There are no goals, no time constraints, no stress. Just being. Interspersing this exercise throughout the session offers an opportunity for quiet regrouping and personal reflection. Here, the horse and the client are doing their magic; the less we do the better.

Ask nothing; require nothing; simply allow yourself to experience the pleasure and comfort of each other's presence. Just being, not doing. So difficult for us Western souls! Before you enter the round pen, get centered. Breathe. Open your heart.

Nothing is required of either of you. Whatever you feel like doing, go ahead. You can join him as he meanders around the field or stand quietly with him as he munches on grass. Or, you might choose to lean on the horse and let him hold the weight of you for a while or breathe quietly with him. Know that he is aware of you without feeling any compunction to interact with you. Perhaps you feel the same. It may be that just sharing the same space is enough for both of you, the basis of all loving, respectful relationships.

―――――――――――――――

When I did this final exercise during my training, my horse decided he wanted to visit the guys on the other side of the fence. So the four of us, heads hanging over the railing, two on one side, two on the other, just hung around; happy to be in each other's company. It was ridiculously relaxing. How lovely it would be to just graze with a few close friends, simply content in their presence, with no pressure to talk or perform or entertain. I felt complete.

In Sum, Chapter Seven covers our all-too-human tendency to take ourselves way too seriously, shrinking our worthiness to a series of overly rehearsed self-criticisms. Being resilient, being self-forgiving, and being generous with your time and love allows us to experience life with a sense of joy and playful curiosity. Horses, who live in the here and now, who meander through their lives with a child-like sense of curiosity (after they decide they are safe), who find ways around obstacles like that newly fallen branch along the trail, and who model contentment and serenity are the perfect therapists for this work!

PART II

TARGET POPULATIONS AND THE BUSINESS OF EQUINE THERAPY

Chapter Eight

Special Populations: A Very Abrieviated Introduction to the Art of Psychological Diagnosis and Treatment Planning[11]

There is no need to get an advanced degree in psychology to practice equine psychotherapy; however it is a good idea to have some basic understanding of what a psychiatric diagnosis can tell you and how it impacts treatment planning.[12]

Basically, an individual is given a diagnosis based on his or her psychological history and current presenting problems. Usually, a psychologist, psychiatrist, or MSW, all of whom are credentialed professionals in their respective states, are responsible for determining a diagnosis. An original diagnosis is like a research hypothesis; it can be modified and/or changed as more is learned on an ongoing basis about the client. Sometimes, a psychiatrist, or a treating clinician, will suggest medication.

---

[11]   I have chosen the diagnostic categories based on my academic and clinical training combined with my experiences in EEP. These categories are fairly complex and often overlapping. Use them simply as a guide in thinking about your clients and how they can be best served. There are excellent books and resources that go into much more detail than I have. This section could be the beginning of a deeper exploration for you. For more detailed information on differential diagnosis, refer to the Diagnostic and Statistical Manual (DSM-5) published by the American Psychiatric Association. I have included the ICD-10 numbers associated with each diagnosis. These numbers are used to indicate the exact diagnosis.

[12]   I have purposely not included Autism in this section. Autism is well served in the excellent mounted-work, disability programs. If you feel that you can use the kind of model described in the book with this population, that's great!

This decision is again dependent on the information gleaned by the clinician at intake and as the client's treatment progresses.

Each diagnosis has a range of severity associated with it, as well as a variety of symptoms. There is a wide variance in each category, and every individual presents differently. Again, diagnoses are constructs subject to revision not hard and fast facts.

A diagnosis is assigned for the sole purpose of creating a treatment plan and to facilitate communication with other treating physicians. It is *not* a label or something we do to stigmatize or punish a client.

Various diagnostic categories often have overlapping emotional and behavioral issues, thereby allowing us to use similar interventions regardless of the working diagnosis. For example, boundary setting exercises can be used for any individual who has been abused, experienced trauma and betrayal, dealt with co-dependency issues, and/or has trouble setting limits. Mindfulness training would be appropriate for any individual dealing with trauma, anxiety, disassociation, addictions, compulsions and obsessions, and any other issues that deals with hyper-stimulation of the nervous system. Your job is to select the equine experiences that might be most beneficial and healing for those individuals who come to you for help.

The relationship with the horse is paramount. No matter what the presenting issues are, no significant and lasting change can happen without an environment of trust, dependability, consistency, unconditional positive regard, acceptance, patience, and kindness.

A Note to the Psychotherapist

Although you have partnered with an equine specialist, you owe it to yourself, your team, your client, *and* your therapy horse to be familiar with and comfortable around horses in general. This means spending hours of time among horses, not just being handed a fully tacked horse for dressage lessons. It would benefit you to get down and dirty, or dusty as the case might be, with your equine co-therapists. Spend a couple of hours literally hanging out with the horses in their paddocks. They don't say much, but there is a lot going on if you tune in to your horse's channel.

Go for trail rides where the horse gets to have a say. Feel the connection you have with your horse, tune into your internal experience when he is being curious and playful, pay attention to how it feels when he tenses up at a strange object along the trail, and notice what it is like when he picks up energy on the way back to the barn and his buddies. Your horse is going to be your co-therapist; take some time to figure each other out and get to know each other. Just makes horse sense!

The Wounded Soldier – Healing With Horses

Returning home after experiencing a war is a complex challenge. Everyone expects their loved one to be the same person they were before they left, but the soldiers know they will never be that person again. Isolation, shame, depression, guilt and grief often accompany the soldier home, further alienating them from the world, the neighborhood, and the family to which they are returning. Trying to fit in with people who do not share their experiences, losses, or memories, is daunting. There are no words to describe the sense of being irreparably broken, the vacuum of despair where hope used to reside.

Compounding the difficult transition facing many returning veterans is the serious emotional, neurological, and physical problems resulting from their war experiences, such as Post Traumatic Stress Disorder (PTSD) and traumatic brain injuries (TBIs). Many symptoms of both conditions overlap further complicating diagnosis and treatment planning. In both cases, the injuries are often invisible further exacerbating feelings of alienation and isolation.

At a loss for words to describe their experiences and emotions, uncomfortable with other people, overwhelmed by life back home, veterans can often find the peace they long for in the quiet and serenity of a stable. They begin to trust a compassionate horse who accepts them just as they are. Finding a non-demanding, nonjudgmental companion in a horse, nurturing and being nurtured by this relationship, trying new skills in the safety of the barn, regaining a sense of mastery, hope, and perhaps, even laughter, is what equine psychotherapy can offer the returning veteran.

A Special Note About Grief.

It takes courage to grieve, to honor the pain we carry. …In touching the pain of recent and long-held griefs, we come face to face with our genuine human vulnerability, with helplessness and hopelessness. These are the storm clouds of the heart.

The Art of Forgiveness, Lovingkindness, and Peace.
                        Jack Kornfield

So many soldiers come back from their respective wars burdened with complicated and difficult emotions. One that needs special attention is grief. Few survive a war experience without sustaining significant loses, be they emotional as in the loss of a sense of hopefulness and joy, material as in the loss of dear friends and comrades, physical, as in the loss of body integrity, or spiritual as in the loss of a long cherished belief in God and the inherent goodness of the world.

Historically, societies and religions have developed rituals to sanctify the process of grieving. The ancient wisdom of allowing the space and time to grieve has been winnowed down to quick condolence visits and well-meaning Hallmark cards reflecting our hectic, future-oriented world. We encourage the hurt soul to "Get on with it!" to "Soldier on!" How sad for all of us.

Using horses, we can enable our soldiers to share their pain and losses, both privately with their equine buddy or as a healing group ritual, similarly to the exercises we employ for sharing shame or any other painful emotion.

GROUP EXERCISE: A GRIEVING RITUAL

Grieving in the company of your brothers and sisters allows for a communal transformational experience. You are not alone. People are there to share your pain, to share your tears, and support you through this journey of loss and, yes, renewal. For grieving, letting go, makes room in your life for new hopes, new relationships, and new sustaining beliefs to grow. You will emerge from your grief with a wisdom born of pain. You can strive to fill your life with possibility, instead of letting your future be ruled by regret.

1. Have each member of the group write down the loses they have sustained in the war. It could be emotional; the friends they have lost in battle, a sense of hopefulness they used to have about their future, the stability of their marriages, the respect of the people they love, a sense of belonging. It could be physical; the loss of a limb, of cognitive abilities, of former physical stamina. Or spiritual; the loss of a belief in a higher power, the loss of the belief in the inherent goodness of people, the loss of a belief in heaven.

2. Have each of them take their lists and read them to the horse. This can be done privately *or* so that the rest of the group can share in hearing the list.

3. After reading the list, perhaps they would like to hug the horse; spend some time in that hug. Each one can then come back for a group hug.

4. If feasible, have each member of the group plant a small plant or sprig in a garden set aside for this ritual, representing the possibility of growth, perhaps a "Hope Garden." Or, you can invite them to bury their list or shred it and cast it to the wind.

5. At the end of the exercise, make sure the group comes together in whatever way is comfortable for them.

Post-Traumatic Stress Disorder – PTSD [F43.10]

PTSD is a serious emotional disorder which can seriously impact many aspects of a person's overall functioning. PTSD is the result of being a victim of, or bearing witness to, terrifying experiences *outside the parameters of normal human experience*. Traumatic events that could induce PTSD are: rape, child molestation/abuse, natural catastrophes such as earthquakes or destructive hurricanes, combat/war, being the victim of a violent crime or being witness to or victim of terrorist attacks. Surviving the 9/11 terrorist attacks and serving in the wars in the Mid-East are current precipitants of PTSD.

Most people, who experience traumatic events, have a heightened level of stress that resolves with time. However, if the symptoms get worse or last for months or even years and interfere with normal functioning, the diagnosis of PTSD needs to be considered. It is also possible to experience late onset PTSD where the symptoms do not develop till years after the precipitating event.

New advances in neuropsychological imaging technology are allowing us to study the brain of people with PTSD. What is being discovered is that emotional trauma actually changes the neural networks within the brain. For further information on this developing breakthrough, I suggest you read Bessel Van Der Kolk, *The Body Keeps Score: Brain, Mind and Body in the Healing of Trauma.*

PTSD symptoms include: flashbacks, nightmares and severe anxiety, as well as intrusive thoughts about the incident. The flashbacks and nightmares might become so vivid and terrifying that the individual, lost in the trauma memory, could act out violent behaviors that would have been appropriate in a war zone but not at home with their family.

People with PTSD have a heightened startle response. They "spook" easily as do horses on trail. In both cases, this results in an adrenalin surge turning on the fight/flight response. Many of you who have experienced your horse take off at full gallop when startled can empathize with that spike in adrenalin!

Often people with PTSD will become depressed and isolated, shunning human contact. They might turn to drugs or alcohol to self-medicate the pain and anxiety resulting in what is called a dual-diagnosis (having a diagnosis of PTSD *and* substance abuse/dependence). Irritability, hypervigilance, avoidance of any situation that causes discomfort, dissociation, are all characteristics of PTSD.

TREATMENT ISSUES:

What is important to emphasize in treatment planning, is that PTSD is a *stress* disorder; therefore any exercise geared towards stress reduction and control will be applicable.

When developing a treatment plan, one activity can often be used to address a number of problems simultaneously. For example, breathing in sync with a horse can work to lessen anxiety levels, stabilize emotional lability (rapid swings between extreme emotions), and enhance the connection between the horse and the client. Deep, slow breathing is highly effective for lowering overall stress levels and regaining control of limbic responses (See: "Trauma Responses" in Chapter Four). Using deep breathing at the beginning and end of sessions enables the client to enter and exit each session with a sense of mastery and calmness.

Important Considerations When Working With PTSD Clients

Mindfulness, emotional (affect) regulation and stress reduction methods all must be interwoven *throughout the session*. The goal is for your clients, via somatic and cognitive cues, to recognize when they are *beginning* to feel triggered or overwhelmed. Being aware of such cues will alert them to immediately begin grounding techniques as well as taking steps to remove themselves from any disturbing stimuli. For example, if one of the horses begins acting up while in cross ties, this might trigger anxiety and fear in one of your clients. They should be encouraged to find a safe space until the horse calms down. Eventually, the client will be able to stay present and not get overwhelmed when a horse gets antsy.

If your client does enter a flashback/dissociative state, stay calm. Give them space and talk to them softly as you would to a horse that has spooked. Gently remind them of where they are, who you are, and that they're safe. Prompt them, repeatedly, to breathe. They will hear you. Though you might be tempted to hug or soothe a person in distress, *do not touch them.* At this particular moment, they might not recognize you and physical contact of any kind could be terrifying! The flashback *will* pass.

If possible, debrief with the client immediately afterwards to help them determine what triggered the flashback. The rest of the session should be spent in quiet activity to allow for your client's nervous systems to return to normal before leaving the barn.

This might sound highly dramatic; most people with PTSD will not have flashbacks during a session. However, it is a good idea to review Chapter Four's discussion about "Amygdala Hijack" and "Disassociation" so you are prepared for such an eventuality.

Being familiar with your horse enables you to know what will cause him to spook; the same applies to your client. For example, you might know that your horse is terrified of puddles. So you are on alert for the pesky puddles after a heavy rain. You might come to learn that the veteran you are working with is triggered by unanticipated touch. Perhaps they were sexually assaulted during their time in the military. You can be on alert for both puddles *and* anyone innocently coming too close to your client.

Making sure the environment is peaceful and calm helps ensure a positive experience. Try to book sessions when the barn is not full of excited children or too much activity.

"Just Being" with the horse, without structured exercises (after mindfulness and grounding exercises), should be an integral part of each session. Relationships are built on the bedrock of trust, acceptance, and safety. The nonverbal, powerful connection that happens with a horse makes this healing particularly empowering. Here the less the therapist's gets involved, the better.

Over time, once a deep relationship has been established with the horse, shame-based sharing exercises can be incorporated as part of the client's routine. The client gets to experience literally putting all their weight, burdens, and guilt-laden stories on the horse, who willingly accepts them.

Group work can be phased into the sessions. This might begin as simply having a few clients groom their horses at the same time, to eventually sharing feelings and experiences at the end of the session. Games and team building activities can be incorporated. Slowly allowing others into their lives, people who have shared similar experiences and fears, goes a long way in mending isolation and self-denigration.

This population can be encouraged, later in treatment, to begin mounted work with the horse.

Traumatic Brain Injury (TBI) [F02.8x]

Traumatic Brain Injuries (TBIs) are *acquired* brain injuries, differentiating them from *congenital* damage to the brain that can happen in vitro or during the birthing process, such as Cerebral Palsy.

Veterans returning from the recent wars in the Mid-East, have a high probability of having sustained a brain injury during their time in-country. These wars, more than those of the past, have been characterized by the extensive use of Improvised Explosive Devices (IEDs) which lead to a particular form of brain injury often seen in certain boxers or football players. The blast from these weapons causes the brain to be literally thrown around within the skull, like a boxer getting repeatedly punched in the head. The damage might also be the result of pressure waves passing through the brain disrupting brain function. The more of these types of injuries the soldier sustains, the more pervasive the brain injury and the poorer the prognosis.

Given the repeated deployments of military personnel during the recent series of wars, the odds of soldiers sustaining multiple brain injuries from IEDs are high.

Traumatic brain injury can have a negative impact on the overall functioning of the individual affecting cognitive, emotional and somatic functioning.

Cognitive Processing:

There is new and hopeful research indicating that the brain can generate new neural pathways to compensate for those that have been destroyed. However, for the sake of treatment planning, we still need to work with the assumption that most brain deficits caused by trauma might be permanent, though perhaps minimized over time. Individuals with TBIs may often encounter the following cognitive difficulties: [13]

- Short term memory is usually seriously impacted. The client might have difficulty remembering appointments, names, horses, what transpired in the last session, etc. For this reason *it is essential* to encourage the client to take notes. This not only helps to orient and prepare them for the next activity on the agenda, but it is also excellent training in compensatory strategies to be used in daily living. The notes might include the steps involved in each activity and what equipment will be needed, such as a bridle, lunge line, and/ or grooming instruments

- Remembering and following sequences. The client might have trouble recalling the order of the steps used in everyday stable tasks, such as which brush to use first when grooming. Again, relying on written notes is important in helping the client act autonomously and in developing a sense of independence and mastery.

- Organization. As with Attention Deficit Disorder, people with TBIs tend to have problems with organization. Each activity will flow more seamlessly if all the equipment is laid out beforehand. Once the client gets used to taking

---

[13]   As we will discuss shortly, both AD/HD and TBIs are both brain injuries. In both cases, the brain has difficulty processing information

notes and becomes more familiar with the layout of the barn and where the equipment is stored, this preplanning can be eased out.

- Maintaining attention and concentration to the task at hand. Similar to the challenges faced by AD/HD clients, people with TBIs are often easily distracted. In such cases, lunging is a perfect exercise in offering immediate feedback. When attention and concentration waver, the horse stops. Maintaining the connection with the horse, getting the horse to keep going, is a wonderful reinforcement technique.

- Impulsive behavior. As we know, sudden movements make horses anxious. For example, if a client becomes frustrated and tosses the lead line down in disgust, it is pretty much guaranteed that the horse will get startled and react. Pretty rapid feedback! This allows the client a real-time opportunity to experience the effect of his impulsive acting out behavior on others around him.

- Language processing issues: TBIs often result in problems understanding words (receptive aphasia) and verbalizing thoughts (expressive aphasia). In addition, someone with a brain injury might perseverate (get stuck on a theme). With all of the above, gentle and consistent feedback and cuing during the actual session with the horse are required. Patience and encouragement are essential to healing. The repetition of terms and procedures will help with language acquisition and expression. All of the above works toward enabling the client to regain a sense of competency and mastery.

- Because of language processing difficulties, nonverbal communication and interactions between the client and the horse becomes that much more meaningful.

- Speed of Processing: Cognitive process might become slower and more arduous after a TBI. Familiarizing the client to tasks via repetition helps increase processing speed. "Slow and steady." It is also an excellent tempo when working with horses.

- Stimuli overload: It is often difficult for the brain injured person to be able to filter out distracting stimuli in the environment. It benefits everyone to schedule sessions during the times when the stable is quiet and peaceful. After school or on weekends, when there might be lots of little children running around and people and horses converging in all directions, might not be the optimal time to work with this population.

In all the above situations, one of our major goals is to increase the client's sense of self-efficacy, mastery, autonomy, and self-respect. More complicated tasks can be assigned as the client masters the basics of each activity.

You might notice the overlap between brain injury behaviors and those of children with AD/HD. They are both reflective of brain issues, both structural (actual damage to the brain as happens in TBIs) and dynamic (processing issues resulting from brain abnormalities as is found in AD/HD). The techniques you apply to AD/HD clients can easily be adapted for those with brain injury and vice versa.

Emotional Issues:

People with TBIs tend towards frustration and impatience when confronted with any problems or setbacks. It is therefore essential to invest time instilling and practicing stress reducing techniques, such as grounding, mindfulness and deep breathing *before* beginning any formal therapy. Simply being around a horse and, perhaps grooming him, is a good place to start developing a strong, trusting relationship.

The following is a list of emotional and behavioral issues that you might face when dealing with a client with TBIs.

- Emotional lability. This signifies the tendency for an individual to rapidly swing from one emotion to another. For example, you might notice your client quickly shifting from patience to anger or calmness to deep frustration. Dramatic displays of emotions, such as crying or yelling, might become the norm. People close to the injured person often report that their loved ones are different people than they remember. Emotional lability is often the cause.

- Frustration. The inability to perform simple tasks can create a high level of frustration and distress as the client remembers what he or she used to be able to do easily but now struggles with.

- Aggression/Irritability. Given the high level of frustration combined with lowered affect regulation, your client might become aggressive and angry when faced with perceived failure.

- Impulsivity. Combining the above two responses can create a potentially dangerous situation, both for the client and those around him, given the brain-injured person's difficulties in maintaining control when overwhelmed by emotions.

- Denial/lack of awareness. Often the brain injured individual is unaware or in denial about their deficits, making therapy that much more challenging.

- Depression and suicidal ideation. It is imperative that all clinicians and people close to the client maintain awareness of the client's level of hopelessness and sense of helplessness. Resource numbers should be kept available in case there is an escalation in depressive symptoms.

- Anxiety. Anxiety is a common symptom of people with TBIs. Clients often feel overwhelmed and not in control of their lives. Any technique that lowers somatic responses, such as deep breathing and mindfulness, should always be employed if the anxiety level begins to heighten.

- PTSD complications. Given the emotional sequelae of brain injury, it is apparent that these issues can exacerbate problems associated with PTSD, specifically angry outbursts, irritability, and periods of confusion and frustration. It is difficult differentiating between the causes of various disabling problems. However, the treatment for them is basically the same. Clients who also have TBIs will need more structure, cuing, organizational aids, and time.

Somatic Issues:

There are numerous medical issues associated with TBIs. It would be the decision of the treating physician to target which issues need to be addressed. For example, often brain injuries manifest as sleep disorders, chronic pain, exhaustion, physical paralysis/spasticity, or seizures. In these cases, it is also useful to consult the treating physician, physical therapist and/or occupational therapist in developing treatment interventions and objectives.

In particular, the treating equine therapists must be aware of any seizure disorders which are not uncommon after TBIs. There should be specific instructions and emergency numbers available if the client were to experience a seizure during a session. Most seizures resolve fairly quickly on their own, and the only requirement is to clear the area so that the client cannot hurt themselves. However, some seizures do not remit quickly, and they need immediate medical attention. In either case, any seizure necessitates a call to a doctor and the client's emergency contact.

Chronic Traumatic Encephalopathy (CTE)

CTE is a very serious, progressive, degenerative disease found in people with a history of repetitive brain trauma.

CTE was initially labeled "dementia pugilistica" (DP), or more colloquially, punch drunk, since it was originally found in boxers. Any athlete who is exposed to repetitive brain injury is at risk to develop this disease. A classic case of it can be seen in Mohammad Ali. It is one of the reasons that has recently motivated parents to prohibit their children from playing football.

It might take years or even decades for CTE to manifest in dementia. As with other TBIs, the symptoms are often memory loss, aggression, confusion, and depression. Unlike other TBIs, this disease is progressive and will lead to a pervasive dementia. To date, there is no way to diagnose CTE except posthumously.

In terms of treatment planning, since there is no way of determining the likelihood of someone developing CTE, all TBI issues should be addressed similarly.

Children and Adolescents

Children and teenagers are classes onto themselves. So much is changing so quickly for them that it is hard to keep up with which issues are the most pressing and at what time. What is true for both subsets is that language is a barrier, as opposed to a vehicle, for communicating concerns, feelings, worries, etc. Young children simply do not have the words necessary to express their feelings, and adolescents refuse to use them. Horses are perfect; they enable these children and teenagers to be heard, understood, and appreciated in a nonverbal, nonjudgmental, and compassionate manner.

Children:

Firstly, they are little! So ponies and miniature horses work best with this miniature population. It is up to the treating therapist, in conjunction with the client's parents, to decide how old the child should be before beginning equine experiential psychotherapy. Before age six might be pushing things a bit for this form of equine therapy. Working with children with physical disabilities or spectrum disorders such as autism does not have the same age constraints of equine psychotherapy.

Remember that young children's attention spans are short and their cognitive skills are still not fully formed, therefore exercises should be chosen with that in mind. All instruction and feedback should be presented in a simple manner. Short sentences, concrete instructions encompassing no more than three steps at a time, and vocabulary equivalent to their developmental level need to be employed when dealing with little humans.

No matter what the presenting issue, there are standard practices to be followed in *each* session. Structure, boundaries, and rules are important when working with children *and* horses! Children thrive in dependable, stable, routinized situations where they can learn to count on certain activities to be repeated weekly. Think how many times they love the same story to be told or read to them….ad infinitum! Many children with emotional issues come from chaotic backgrounds, be it recent divorce, parental illness, addiction, abuse, or simply overwhelmed, overstressed families. Having a tranquil place to be each week where they can trust that everything remains the same is in itself very healing.

The barn should have a quiet place assigned to the children. This area will be where the children go to meet their therapists, leave their book bags, snacks, etc. and where they return to after their sessions to "debrief." It is advisable to have some toys (stuffed ponies?), books and drawing material in that area. The cozier and warmer, the better.

Children might prefer to draw their feelings as opposed to talk about them. Drawing, in itself, is very therapeutic, and they can take the pictures home to remind them of what they learned and accomplished and/or shared with their therapists.

PROTOTYPICAL EQUINE THERAPY SESSION WITH CHILREN

An adult should be present at all times during the equine work. However it would be beneficial to give the child enough space and privacy that they can freely "talk" to their horse friend.

Each session should start with a review of safety rules. Over time, the children can remember and recite these rules by themselves, thereby starting off with a sense of accomplishment and familiarity.

- The children can greet the therapy horse in whatever way they like, maybe a hug, or a "hello"? They might want to share with their horse friend how their week went. In addition, asking the horse how he or she is feeling reinforces empathy and the awareness of others.
- The children then retrieve their grooming kits (each child gets to choose a grooming kit at the first session, different colors would be nice!) and begin grooming their horses.

- A period of resting on the horse should follow the grooming. This is the equivalent of "quiet time" for both the horse and the child. This also reinforces safe connection.

- Each child gets to choose the activity of the day. Remember, this is about bonding, safety and relationship building, so the activity can be basically anything the child feels comfortable doing.

Gender Specific Approaches (this is not PC, but it is real).

Little girls often like playing make believe and "dress up" with their horse friend. Boas and hats seem to be the favorite of the small, feminine set, and horses usually don't mind being gussied up. The stories they make up are often reflective of the issues in their lives and should be noted (eavesdropping is allowed) and recorded for the treating therapist. This is the EEP equivalent of Play Therapy.

For example, a little girl might have imaginary friends over for tea with her horse boyfriend. She might get very upset if the horse is distracted or appears to be more interested in something going on in the barn rather than playing with her. She might withdraw and sulk. Or get angry at the horse. Perhaps she is longing for sustained and nourishing attention from Mommy and Daddy who might be distracted by a new baby brother or sister, overwhelmed by work and family, or constantly on the cell phone. She doesn't yet know how to get the focused attentiveness she craves.

The therapist might ask her, "How does it feels to have the horse ignore you?" (Angry? Hurt? Sad?) A corollary question would be, "Where in your body do you feel that anger or hurt?" I bet it is in her belly…this is where little kids seem to hold emotions. How many times do we hear, "My belly hurts!" when there is something scary looming in the future, such as a test or the first day of school. What they are asking for is a hug and reassurance.

What might she say to her horse boyfriend to explain how hurt it makes her feel when she thinks she's being ignored? "Can you tell the horse what you feel? What you need? What would that be like? Why not try it?" Of course, now it is up to you to make sure the horse pays attention to her...that's where spontaneous creativity pays off!

When the horse once again is focused on her and the game, you can ask her how she feels *now,* using her words and noticing her body.

At the end of the exercise, you might go over what she learned. Could she use the same feeling words with her mother and father as she did with the horse? You might ask her what she thinks might happen if she tried. You could rehearse with her and reinforce the importance of using her "feelings" words.

Little boys can do dress-up games too but sometimes they prefer, and are more comfortable with, action-oriented activities. Fantasy is still key here. If they want to play space aliens with the horse or Batman, or whatever the latest Disney fad is, go for it! Remember, their play is not only therapeutic, as they act out their issues in their choice of roles and actions, but the story they create is very telling. Of course, the way they relate to the horse is very important. Is the horse an ally? An enemy? How is the horse treated? As an equal? Subserviently? Little kids are always telling a story, if we know how to listen.

For example, if a little boy is being too pushy and aggressive with the horse (which of course is not allowed and must be redirected), he might be expressing his experience of being belittled and powerless in his home or being bullied at school. That could be explored during the activity. Corrective actions could be suggested. "What would happen if the 'hero' spoke up for himself or went for help from an adult?" "How would that feel?"

{Note: It is perfectly okay to share what you are learning about your client with their treating therapist. This is where having a HIPPA form on file becomes important. We will discuss HIPPA regulations later in the book.}

After their activity, it is time to wrap up the session. Remember, these are little kids, and their attention span is short. Have them say goodbye to their horse and thank them. Ask them what the horse said to them in return.

Once you are both back in the children's area having snacks, invite them to share their feelings and what they learned today. It would be helpful to have a Feelings Chart to cue them as to the different emotions they might have experienced. Include asking them how they thought the horse felt.

If they like, they can do some drawings about their experiences. These are always good to send back to their treating therapists who can use the content for further discussion. Or, simply, to hang on their wall to remember the events of that day

Child Abuse Victims

Children who have experienced abuse or have been witness to abuse need special gentleness and attention.

Ethical responsibility is essential when treating children who have been abused. If you feel as if the child is in danger, you *must* contact the therapist and/or authorities immediately. Children count on us to keep them safe. If there is or might be a court case pending regarding the welfare of the child, then you need to make sure that detailed notes of each session are maintained; they might be requisitioned by a court. Again, you will need a HIPPA form signed by the parent or whichever adult is making decisions for the child.

Certain considerations are particularly important when working with children who have been abused.

- At the beginning of treatment, the child might be highly mistrustful of adults. It is best to leave them alone with a pony or miniature horse with minimal instructions thereby enabling them to bond in their own ways and at their own speed.

- Attention must be paid if the child acts out his or her anger or attempts to reenact the abuse that might have been witnessed or endured. Children tend to literally act out what they are scared of, trying to gain a sense of mastery over a frightening world. If this happens, of course, stop the child and ask him or her to tell the horse how he or she feels. In this case using words, instead of actions, is obviously the better choice.

- One-on-one games, appropriate to your client's developmental level, can be incorporated as therapy progresses. This can include reading to the horse, dressing the horse up, having the horse join in an adventure such as space exploration (roaming the paddock...). Remember, fun and laughter are important ingredients to healing; nothing is as gratifying as a child's laughter. And horses enjoy a good game as much as anyone!

- Information might be gleaned from your session that might be important to share with the child's therapist. Or the authorities, if ongoing abuse is suspected.

- As with all other children's barn activities, structure and dependable routines are essential. These give the child a sense of order, predictability, and safety in an otherwise very scary world, whether they have been abused or are living in a chaotic household.

Ethical, Legal, and Parental issues dealing with Child Equine Assisted Therapy

The barn should always have on file:

- Consent and release forms from the responsible adults. This includes the HIPPA form which permits the equine and mental health therapists to share their work with the child's primary therapist, parent, or school representative.

- A medical history and emergency contacts, including any medication or medical issues that would need to be attended to, e.g. seizure disorders, AD/HD, allergies, etc.

- The original report from the referring clinician including a diagnosis and behavioral/emotional goals. This report might also be generated from the children's school or referring agency.
- A Progress Report/Treatment History. Logging in the day's activities and findings will enable smooth continuity of treatment from week to week.

It is recommended that the parents, or whomever brings the child, remain in the barn for the hour session. The benefit is twofold. Since these are small children, they might need to be reassured by their parents during any part of the session. Also, this avoids having parents not available on time to pick up their children. Amazing, but this is a common issue! No one wants bored little children running around the stable!

Adolescents:

Adolescents are a horse of a different color! They have perfected the art of stonewalling any adult who tries to pry any information out of them. Asking "What's new?" "How's school?" "How are you feeling?" can be an exercise in utter frustration. The proverbial conversation with a brick wall would sometimes be more gratifying.

It is upsetting and exacerbating for parents to be aware that their beloved child is having problems, (e.g. their grades are dropping, they are isolating, they refuse to eat, and they are argumentative and grouchy) and be at a loss as to why this is happening and how to help. Working with adolescents is tough on a therapist, too. Unlike small children, adolescents have the words, but they refuse to tell Any Adult, including therapists, *anything*. Not only would you "Not understand" but you, being an adult, are by definition not trustworthy. Add to that resistance the fact that most adolescents would rather be anywhere else but in a therapist's office.

As disconcerting as this is for the adults, it is that much more painful for adolescents. They are going through so many biological and physical changes: raging with hormones, grieving the safety of childhood (though not consciously), attempting to break away from their parents and desperately trying to bond with their peer group.

They have yet to learn the skills needed to cope with the blizzard of changes and demands descending on them. Of course, it does not help that they think they are "perfectly fine" and that their parents are nuts.

Adolescents are a group precariously balanced on the brink of adulthood and unsure as to whether they are up to the task. They tend to be impulsive, impressionable, easily bruised, scared, and desperate to be accepted by their peers. Their poor judgment, combined with impulse control issues, often places them in risky and dangerous situations. This is a perfect population to benefit from equine therapy.

Horses to the Rescue!

The basic goals of equine therapy with adolescents are to help teens take responsibility for their actions, learn to communicate effectively, set boundaries, trust and respect themselves, slow down and make thoughtful decisions, and to create healthy, respectful relationships.

Dealing with overwhelming emotions, such as anger, loneliness, self-loathing, insecurity, and depression, without getting flooded with anxiety, is a major task of this developmental stage. All too often, adolescents will either act out or shut down. Acting out can take the form of alcohol and drug use, problems with the law, running away, and/or engaging in damaging, destructive relationships. Shutting down can result in the teen's isolation, avoidance, serious depression, eating disorders, self-mutilation, suicide attempts, etc. The list continues.

When working with adolescents, it is often recommended to start with individual equine therapy. The immediate goal is to create a space where the teen can take off the persona of "coolness" and just be real with the horse in a nonjudgmental atmosphere. As with little children, it is a good idea to give the adolescent some space to work out a relationship with their horse without adults nudging them.

Eventually, group activity in the form of "play" can be added when the teen is better able to hold onto a sense of who they are without succumbing to the adolescent imperative of fitting in.

Group activity allows the teen to experience cooperation with others - setting common goals, learning to compromise, developing compassion, belonging to and being accepted by a peer group just as they are, and just plain having fun! It is okay to laugh at yourself or the antics of others; it is safe to lose yourself in the joy of the game. Entering adulthood is scary but you still get to play!

PROTOTYPICAL EQUINE THERAPY SESSION WITH ADOLESCENTS

Warning: The less pressure put on the adolescent to talk, the better! Asking a teen how he or she "feels" is guaranteed to shut them down faster than a surprise quiz.

- As with any client, each therapy session should have a routine so that the teen knows where to find their grooming material and can begin the hour by grooming their horse independently.
- Allow the adolescent to be as autonomous as possible. Hopefully, by the end of each session, decisions were made as to what would be worked on this week. You can check in with the teen to see if this activity is still alright with them.
- Any of the exercises in the book can be used with the adolescent. If, however, your client refuses to do anything (not an uncommon occurrence with a teenager) make sure that they remain in the paddock with the horse for the duration of the session. A lead line, some horse toys, etc. might be "left" in the paddock in case the teen becomes inspired to interact with the horse. So much happens when we leave people alone with horses; oftentimes, the less we intervene the better. Of course, a therapist should be keeping an eye on the action (or non-action) in the paddock.
- You might risk congratulating your client when they have accomplished something new and challenging. Perhaps they were able to get the horse to

walk with them at liberty (a lovely feeling that someone *actually* wants to be with him or her!). Maybe a boundary was set that the horse respected. Perhaps the teen successfully lunged the horse at all gaits and had the horse come for a nuzzle at the end of the exercise. What great teamwork! And to feel loveable? Who wouldn't appreciate having a nice lick at the end of a difficult task?

- At the end of the session, you can *try* to debrief with the adolescent. At a minimum, you can ask your client to write down in their journal the experience(s) they had during the session and in what ways this might come in useful during the upcoming week. Painting, clay sculpting, writing – all are possible paths to expression.

- Once you feel that the adolescent would benefit from group activities, any of the "fun" group exercises can be used. You might prepare the client for the upcoming group experience by asking what they imagine that might be like. What about it might be stressful? How might it be fun? Hopefully, by this time, your client will not look at you as a predator, since you haven't eaten him yet, and be willing to actually talk about feelings and concerns. Group experiences are not only useful for their interpersonal challenges, but also for practicing problem-solving, resiliency, and frustration tolerance. With teens, their peers are often their most critical mirror and yet their most appreciated audience.

Of course, as with child therapy, ongoing note taking by the equine specialist and/or therapist is imperative.

Attention Deficit/Hyperactivity Disorder [F90.8][14]

Brain abnormalities, whether acquired (e.g. TBIs) or congenital (AD/HD) present with comparable behavioral and emotional characteristics and so treatment goals are frequently similar for these differing conditions. Many of the equine exercises we discussed to address TBI issues can be employed when working with AD/HD. Attention Deficit/Hyperactivity Disorder (AD/HD), which is usually diagnosed

---

14   The most recent DSM-5 now labels ADD and ADHD as AD/HD.

as a result of a child's behavioral and academic issues in school, presents as both a cognitive *and* behavioral disorder.

Cognitive processing problems revolve around the difficulty of maintaining attention and concentration. Children with AD/HD tend to be easily distracted by outside stimuli and are often described as being "in a cloud" or daydreaming or the opposite, in perpetual motion. They struggle with details, organization, and sequential processing. Avoiding challenging tasks becomes a way of coping with the sense of chronic failure.

Behaviorally, these children can be highly agitated, antsy (cannot sit still), impulsive, and/or disruptive in a classroom setting. They might compensate by being the "class clown." Or, they can be so quiet, that they almost disappear.

Interpersonally, children with AD/HD often lack the subtle social cues needed to successfully navigate relationships. They are innocently pushy, impatient, talk over others, and have a difficult time maintaining the necessary interpersonal connections needed to develop compassion and empathy for others. Again, the opposite might be true. They might be loners, avoiding all interpersonal interactions. Often, children with AD/HD grow up into adults with AD/HD. These adults, though having developed compensatory skills, can still struggle with interpersonal issues that do not resolve with age.

It is useful, when working with this population, to ask the referring school and/or therapist for specific behavioral goals, e.g. working with the client to increase attention span, lower fidgeting behavior, lower distraction to outside stimuli, etc.

Working with horses enables someone with AD/HD to:

- Learn to stay focused and on task (paying attention to what is going on here and now). Horses will quickly alert you when you have "spaced out" and lost connection with them. They walk away. What keeps a horse connected is a constant flow of energy that requires ongoing concentration. Without that, he would rather go play with his buddies or eat stray pieces of hay. The inability to sustain concentration on a task is a hall mark of AD/HD and will require patience on the part of the therapist and the horse! Slow and steady progress in this area is the goal.

- Deal with frustration, disappointment, and anger. Wanting immediate results, and not getting them, can cause a lot of angst to someone struggling with AD/HD. Horses will not be pushed! Being able to help the client slow down, recognize and deal with feelings, and lower the impulsive rush to action, are all significant milestones. Horses are wonderful at reflecting the emotional energy emanating from a person. The quieter and calmer the person becomes, the quieter and calmer the horse.

- Learn to "listen" to the horse's response. Being able to slow down, attend to, and read the emotional cues emanating from others, *and* wait your turn to talk are difficult skills for someone with AD/HD. These abilities are necessary to develop and sustain relationships, with people and horses! For example, failing to notice that the horse you are trying to pet has his ears flat back on his head and is snorting loudly, might end up with you getting a nasty nibble! These are obvious cues that the horse is getting annoyed with your attempts at affection. Time to step back and give him space. If a horse nudges you playfully, that is an invitation to come closer. Noticing is the key!

- Follow directions. Attending to and following through on the various steps needed to complete equine tasks, such as grooming or putting on a halter, and to sustain the activity to completion, are key cognitive components that are often difficult for the AD/HD client.

- Organize their environment. Dealing with the various pieces of equine equipment, keeping them neat and orderly and putting them back in the order in which they were originally arranged, all call for organizational skills.

Any of the exercises in the book can be used for cognitive retraining therapy with the emphasis on addressing attentional deficits, impulsivity, disorganization, lack of empathy, and any other characteristics that are concurrent with a diagnosis of AD/HD.

Cat therapy for AD/HD husbands. My wonderful husband has quite a case of AD/HD, which he will never acknowledge. Watching him in action in social settings can be almost painful! He talks over other people, changes the topic if someone is speaking about something that does not interest him, or simply spaces out if the attention isn't focused on him or some stimulating topic, such as the stock market. Finally, I had him sit on the carpet with me and our two cats, Fanny and Walter, who were very chatty felines. "Watch, Bob. First one cat will meow, and then the other will meow. They don't meow at the same time and drown the other's meow out or cut the other's meow short!" Well, it worked. Whenever we were in a social situation, I was able to cue him by whispering "meow" in his ear.

Equine Therapy and Addiction

Addiction is a highly complex issue encompassing everything from psychological addictions, such as compulsive gambling to biological dependence on a drug like alcohol or heroine. All addictions create a temporary sense of euphoria and/or a release from pain and distress. Once the mood altering effect of the substance or compulsive behavior wears off, the person is left in a state of withdrawal and discomfort, leading to further addictive behavior.

What characterizes all addicts is the dependence on *something outside of themselves* to create and maintain a sense of inner peace. This progresses to a state of chronic dependency on that external object, whether that is a line of cocaine, a piece of chocolate, or a sexual encounter with a stranger.

There are a number of psychological characteristics shared by the majority of people suffering from addictions. The following is a list of common emotional issues:

- The overuse of intellectual defenses to explain and justify their addictions, such as denial that there is anything amiss, projection of blame onto other(s) for all their problems, and/or empty promises that they will "change tomorrow."

- An inability to tolerate strong, uncomfortable emotions without numbing their discomfort with their addiction of choice reflecting a lack of coping skills and an intolerance of strong emotions.

- A propensity to become easily frustrated and enraged by everyday stress and/ or problematic interpersonal issues.

- A lack of empathy and compassion for oneself and as well as others.

- A deep sense of inadequacy, often masked behind a bravado persona.

- A false and precariously held belief that they can control everything and everyone in their lives, including the addictive substance.

- Shame cycles that motivate and reinforce the addictive behavior. Promises to oneself and others that they will stop, followed by relapse leading to intolerable levels of shame and self-denigration, leading to further promises and further relapse.

Equine experiential psychotherapy can be particularly effective in addressing the above issues.

Recovery is based on the Serenity Prayer: *God grant me the serenity to accept the things I cannot change, the courage to change the things I can, and the wisdom to know the difference.*[15] This is one of the most difficult, humbling and healing descriptions of living a sober life. Enter our therapy horse to help the recovering individual understand, in a physical and visceral manner, the power of this prayer.

Horses and Addiction Recovery

The immediacy of every interaction with a horse demands concentration and attention to what is happening *right now*. Maintaining a mindful stance is a significant challenge to a newly recovering individual who is often struggling with

---

[15]   Your own, personal higher power does not have to be of a religious nature.

major neurological and emotional changes. However, *not attending to* a 1000+ pound, huge animal standing directly in front of you is pretty nigh impossible.

Add in some humility. No one can really control a horse. You *can* ask the horse, in a respectful manner, to work with you. Watching a horse expert *appear to* make a horse to do his or her bidding, is really witnessing the power of non-verbal communication based on mutual respect, trust, understanding and appreciation. Horse people have gained the wisdom to know the difference between what they can control, (their own actions and feelings), what they cannot control, (a thousand+ pound animal), and have found the wisdom to come to peace with this reality. Based on that, and with loving kindness to both the self and the horse, all things are possible.

Masking your anxiety and fear behind a bravado, aggressive demeanor backfires when dealing with a highly sensitive animal, such as a horse, who might very well respond with his own aggression. No one seems brave when confronted with an angry, challenged horse. Nothing is quite as humbling! You cannot control a horse, accept that and life becomes oh so much pleasanter for all concerned. You can ask but you cannot tell a horse what to do!

Neither will a horse buy into someone's artificial charm, defensive passivity, or overlearned attempts at caretaking. Horses, by nature, have a very low tolerance for inauthenticity, poor boundaries, and emotional incongruity. Honesty, with oneself and others, is the only game in town, or in this case, the barn.

In other words, you cannot "control" a horse, just as you cannot control your addiction. Both are more powerful than you are. However, you can begin to have a relationship with a horse where control is preempted by respect, trust and caring. Being humble before the power of a horse is not being a wimp. It takes tremendous courage to face something bigger than you…and admit it.

Horses will never judge you, never shame you, and never ask of you what you cannot give. A horse will accept you as the flawed, complex, yet inherently worthwhile person you are. If you try, they will try. If you respect them, they will, in turn, respect you. Words are not needed, just the quietness of your heart and the openness of your spirit.

Treatment Planning

The following is a review of the relevant issues that need to be incorporated in treatment planning when working with addictions.

First and foremost, all treatment will be futile if the addict is still "active" in his or her addiction. This might be difficult to assess since someone in the throes of addiction might be highly skilled at hiding and/or denying the problem. Addiction recovery is often characterized by "slips," relapse often being part of the recovery process. It is therefore important to maintain close contact with the referring individual or organization who might be more privy to the struggles the client might be having in staying sober.[16]

Secondly, many addicts often have what is labeled as a "dual diagnosis," such as alcohol addiction *and* depression. It is imperative that the addiction be addressed first; there is no healing from emotional issues if the person is still actively using his or her substance of choice thereby avoiding or masking all other issues.

Thirdly, all addictions are not the same. Different addictions and compulsions attract people with specific personality types and underlying emotional issues. Treatment has to be planned accordingly. Each treatment plan must reflect a good understanding of the specific issues of a client's addiction *and* his or her individual issues, strengths, history and hopes.

Stages of Recovery:

There are often three different stages in addiction recovery, each of which requires differing therapeutic interventions.

---

[16]   There are various ways to determine if a person has returned to their addiction. It is beyond the scope of this book to describe them. However, if you notice any change in attitude, an increase in absenteeism, or a marked increase in anger or frustration, it is prudent to check with the client's referring therapist.

- *The first stage* is the actual physical withdrawal from the drug of choice, be it alcohol, heroine, OxyContin, etc. This phase is called Detoxification, "detox" in common parlance. Detox occurs in a medical setting where the addict can get the medical support they need to safely withdraw from the addictive substance. Needing to be hospitalized during detox usually depends upon the nature, degree, and duration of a person's addiction. Most addicts will not need a hospital based detox.

- *The second stage* is referred to as "Early Sobriety." Early sobriety is a critical time during which the client is the most fragile and most as risk for relapse. The addict is dealing with rapid emotional and physical changes that can be overwhelming and highly discomforting. Support, encouragement, and practical help are required as the recovering individual learns to negotiate powerful feelings.

A major challenge, during this stage, is helping the client cope with strong emotions without having yet mastered the techniques necessary to deal with these uncomfortable feelings.

- *The third stage* is long-term recovery which is considered a life-long endeavor. The recovering person is beginning to incorporate new strategies, insights, coping mechanisms, and support systems into their lives. They begin to recognize addictive "triggers" and work on accepting responsibility for finding healthier means of dealing with uncomfortable emotions. Over time, understanding and forgiveness of themselves and others develop, and a more trusting and loving person emerges.

There are a multitude of challenges facing an addict, particularly during the first year of sobriety. Equine Experiential Psychotherapy can begin at either the second or third stage of recovery with the goals adjusted to fit the needs of the recovering individual. Fluidity in both treatment planning and goal setting is necessary to reflect the continuous changes inherent in new sobriety.

The First Year of Sobriety

During the early stages of sobriety, the individual will need more support, encouragement, and patience. Lowered frustration tolerance, poor affect regulation (inability to control strong emotions), and increased displays of anger, agitation, and cognitive confusion are to be expected. Remember, the addict's brain is changing rapidly. The nervous system, often having been depressed due to the use of drugs, is now on hyper-drive, causing increased levels of anxiety and hyper-responsiveness. This is particularly true for any of the drugs that depress the nervous system, such as alcohol, heroine or pain medications.

Experiencing strong feelings is unfamiliar and uncomfortable. Up to sobriety, individuals depended upon their drug of choice to deaden feelings of anxiety, insecurity, stress, depression, anger, guilt, and/or shame. Learning to recognize, and then tolerate, powerful emotions presents major challenges during the first year of sobriety

Meanwhile, the addict's family has often become collateral damage in this ongoing war.[17] Hiding behind a façade of perfectionism and grandiosity and masking deep feelings of shame and inadequacy, renders the addict incapable of having open, honest relationships. They are strangers to themselves, how could they be emotionally real with others. As we know, horses will not tolerate this inauthenticity; they are emotional barometers, uncompromisingly honest with their feedback.

Addicts need to "get real" and horses make sure that happens. Horses are truly effective at breaking through the false façade to the truth of a person. Once that person's "truth" is exposed, the compassion and acceptance the horse generates becomes a template of self-forgiveness.

---

[17]   We will be discussing the effects of addiction on the various members of the family in the next section.

Ownership of responsibility, development of trust, and extending respect for self and others are basic interpersonal skills that need to be developed if sobriety and serenity are to be achieved and maintained. Horses are gentle and forgiving teachers. Instinctually, being prey animals, they realize that their herd is only as strong as their weakest member. It is therefore the fragile members of the herd that garner extra love, including damaged, hurting humans.

GROUP EXERCISE –A FEELINGS PRIMER

This exercise can be used with any group where simply recognizing and labeling feelings is a new skill.

- As with all equine sessions, the first steps include: centering via deep breathing, mindfulness, body scans, and grounding exercises. Part of the initial work with a recovering client is recognizing, labeling and locating feelings, from now on referred to as "The Feeling Drill."

- Once everyone is seated in the barn, each member gets to share what they are thinking, how they are feeling, and where they experience that feeling in their body. The horse should be in cross ties near the group thereby including him in the process.

- Each participant then gets the opportunity to express their feelings about the horse (this is a wonderful example of the use of projection) including conjecture about how the horse might be feeling.

- Basic instructions as to how to approach a horse will be reviewed.

- Whoever chooses to can greet the horse via a pet on the horse's neck or with a friendly nose bump. Each step in building a relationship with the horse should be accompanied by the Feeling Drill. Include the horse each time; how do you think he's feeling?

- After some show and tell about grooming, the group can try it on their own. Anyone who is uncomfortable has the option of watching until they feel ready to approach the horse. There is no shame in being scared; it is a basic human emotion, right along with happiness.

GROUP EXERCISE: LETTING GO OF THE ILLUSION OF CONTROL

This exercise is particularly effective with people dealing with addiction. It is also useful for people who use control as a psychological defense against a sense of helplessness or inadequacy. For example, parentified children of dysfunctional families had to assume responsibility for the whole family. This usually was way above their maturity pay grade and often robbed them of their childhood. This exercise playfully challenges their overlearned responses.

- The group enters the ring where the horse will be waiting at liberty. The "game" is to "move" the horse from one end of the ring to the other without touching the horse. Warnings should be issued about loud screaming or rowdy arm waving. If the group is too large, feel free to divide them in half and have them "compete" for how quickly they accomplish the task (or how long it takes them to get exhausted and give up!).

- Next, up the ante. The therapists will create a demarcated area out of whatever is available in the barn. The group now needs to get the horse to enter the designated area. Again, no hands allowed! There are many versions of this exercise, use your imagination!

- Corral your group and bring them back into the stable. Talk about how it felt to try to *control* the horse. Things that might be discussed are:

- How could this concept of "control" be applied to your sobriety? What (and whom) are you trying to control in your life? How is that going? What do you fear would happen if you gave up control?

- Further questions are likely to follow. Did you have to be in charge when growing up? What would have happened if you didn't pick up the ball/assume responsibility for your family? Who was the "controller" in your family? How did they control you? Fear? Guilt? Abdication of parental responsibilities? How did that feel? Do you recognize these manipulative techniques in yourself? How does this feel?

• What are alternative methods of getting your needs met besides control?

After each exercise, allow for group discussion. Encourage exploring how the work they accomplish today could be applied in their lives. Could they think of examples of how letting go of control would change the quality of their relationships? What might be their underlying concerns about letting go of control?

Feel free to create treatment plans incorporating the exercises described in previous sections of the book. All the exercises focusing on developing trust, depending on others to share your burdens, letting go of shame, asking for help, etc. would be applicable.

The Twelve-Step Program

Using the twelve-step program in conjunction with equine psychotherapy is an excellent treatment plan. Much of the twelve-step work is behavioral in nature and task oriented, making it easily adapted to equine experiential psychotherapy.

Each of the twelve steps can be operationalized into an exercise. For example, you can use the exercises on "shame and sharing" to help participants acknowledge and forgive their character defects, practice making amends to people they have hurt, and let go of toxic secrets.

Or have your client try to catch and halter a loose horse in the arena. Nothing teaches humility and acceptance of powerlessness in a more energetic and fun way than chasing a pony who is enjoying the game!

The work of Johnny Higginson and Susan Kelegian at "Saddles and Serenity" Program is an excellent model of incorporating the twelve steps into equine psychotherapy.

Co-Dependency and Family Involvement

Addiction is often referred to as a family disease. Each member of the family is directly impacted in myriad, if not obvious, ways. The character of the family, as a whole, develops around the unacknowledged addiction which assumes center stage. This phenomenon of shared denial is often referred to as tip-toeing around the dinosaur in the living room. It is therefore imperative to incorporate the whole family into the equine psychotherapy treatment. Not only is this therapeutic and educational for the members of addict's family, but it is often the first time the family can engage in healthy, reparative experiences as a unit.

It is often the case that one person, often the spouse or parent of the addict, functions as the enabler of the addict. This individual, the "co-dependent," has protected the addict from the consequences of their addiction, e.g. calling the alcoholic's boss and reporting that their spouse is sick when in truth the individual is too hung-over to go to work or covering bounced checks that have accrued due to the compulsive gambler's debts.

As long as a co-dependent feels indispensable, they feel safe from being abandoned. Another way of maintaining control is for the co-dependent to sabotage the addict's recovery. For example, the husband who brings home a gooey cake when he knows his wife is desperately dieting. Not fair. If she got thin, perhaps she'd leave him. Co-dependents, unsure of their inherent lovability, will settle for being needed.

Equine exercises covering the following topics should be considered when developing a treatment plan for the co-dependent: boundary setting and maintenance, emotional congruence, self-worth and mastery, shame issues, unresolved abandonment issues, and subtle controlling behaviors.

After a certain number of individual sessions, when both the addict and codependent have achieved some level of insight and mastery, couples treatment with the horses can be integrated. Having the couple work together to solve problems, share tasks, respect boundaries (between themselves and the horses), and showing respect and empathy towards each other is a powerful vehicle for growth and change.

These exercises could include the couple moving the horse from one end of the arena to the other, working to build an obstacle course and then maneuvering the horse through it, and any other of the previously described exercises that require team work and communication. These experiences can demonstrate to the co-dependent partner, in real time, how they attempt to "save" the addict from difficult situations. The addict gets to see how they defer decisions to their significant other instead of taking responsibility for their own behavior. If things go wrong, there is always someone else to blame.

Once the couple has had the opportunity to practice new skills and gain insights into their behavior, it might be time to include the rest of the family. Often each child of a family defined by addiction, or some other major dysfunction, assumes a specific role. Some of the more classic roles are: 1) The Perfect Child – the child who does nothing wrong, is totally self-sufficient, gets straight A's, and presents a "normal" façade to the outside world; 2) The Black Sheep – the child who acts out the anger and resentment that underlies the family by getting into trouble with the law, failing at school, using drugs, etc. 3) The Negotiator – the child that runs interference between all warring parties by acting like the diplomat, desperately trying to formalize a truce….for the sake of peace for everyone! Often one of the children gets "parentified" meaning they start to assume the adult responsibilities that their parents are too self-absorbed to assume.

FAMILY EXERCISE: FAMILY ROLES

This exercise can be used with any dysfunctional family. It can also be employed if there is one "identified patient," a child that holds the symptoms of the family.

Before beginning this exercise, the therapist should meet separately with the children and discuss the different roles each child enacts in the family drama. The children get to choose the role they feel *most* represents them. If they have other ideas for roles, go with it. If they don't want to participate, that is okay too. Being "the observer" is also a role.

- Each child gets to create their own sign with their assigned family "role."
- The whole family enters the arena where the therapists will have erected three circles. The goal is for the family team to move the horse from one circle to the next. The horse has to stay in each circle for two minutes. It's up to the therapists if they will allow gently nudging.
- The children should feel free to ham it up, exaggerating their role during the exercise. They can also switch role, if they choose, to share a sibling's experience. Remember, laughter is a wonderful gift, particularly for a family that has been torn apart by the strife of addiction.
- Make sure to debrief with the family about these exercises. These sessions should be serious but there is nothing wrong with having fun and bonding over shared experiences. It is good for the soul!

Before any family activity, you might like to take a lesson from Barbara Rector, the founder and director of Adventures in Awareness (AIA) and truly one of the Wise Women of equine experiential psychotherapy. She starts each session with participants taking the following pledge:

"I agree to be responsible for myself today, and in so doing I contribute to the safety of the group. This means that I am responsible and in charge of my perceptions, my thoughts, my feelings, my emotions and my behavior."

BEING AT WAR WITH YOUR BODY

There exists a myriad of emotional disorders where the individual is at war with their body in self-destructive and often brutal ways. Although it is beyond the scope of this book to go into detail about these disorders, they share enough underlying pathology to begin to delineate a prototypical equine intervention.

First, let's review some of the more common diagnosis. It is important to understand the significant differences and underlying causes of each disorder to be able to create an appropriate treatment plan and therapeutic goals.

Anorexia [F50.8] is a "body distortion" disorder where the individual attempts to achieve and maintain a body mass that she feels is "acceptable" by literally starving her body. People with anorexia perceptually distort their body image. What they see, and what others see when looking at them, often vary enormously. It takes an exceptional amount of self-control and negation of body signals to allow this denial of food to occur. Ceding control and reentering their bodies, becoming friends with their basic needs (hunger), having compassion for their humanness and imperfections, learning to tune into and trust their instincts and animal wisdom, all are key in the healing process.

Body Dysmorphic Disorder (BDD) [F42} is another perceptional distortion disorder. With BDD the person actually sees a terrible, unacceptable imperfection on their bodies which shames and humiliates them. They feel "monstrous." No amount of reassurance can dissuade them that they are not physically repellent.

BDD is a highly debilitating condition which can lead to numerous, unnecessary plastic surgeries (which never really solve the problem), isolation, self-loathing, and self-destructive behaviors.

With both anorexia and BDD, it is often necessary to enlist medication to help the brain begin to resolve the delusional qualities of their body perceptions. These disorders can be life threatening and need to be treated in conjunction with medical guidance.

Binge Eating/Bulimia [F50.2] consists of someone spending inordinate amounts of time ruminating about food and planning a binge where a large amount of food is consumed in a secretive, out of control, and compulsive manner. Once the person is sated, they attempt to purge themselves by inducing vomiting, taking laxatives or extreme exercise.

Self-Mutilation might consist of cutting, compulsive hair pulling, picking at the skin till scabs are formed, and head banging. These are further examples of self-abusive behaviors geared towards ameliorating what is perceived to be intolerable feelings such as self-loathing and shame. Cutting can have the paradoxical effect of allowing someone who feels "dead" or "numb" to physically experience *anything*.

The aforementioned disorders share certain characteristics which makes them amendable to working with horses. Each of the following issues can be dealt with via equine therapy:

- Lack of trust in their own perceptual and somatic experiences.
- Impulse control issues.
- An inability to tolerate uncomfortable feelings.
- Self-loathing, lack of self-compassion and forgiveness.
- Often a history of abuse, either physical and/or sexual.
- Isolation and shame.
- Perceived feelings of powerlessness and helpless. (Cannot control the outside world, but *can* control their bodies.)
- Compulsive rumination leading to an inability to attend to the here and now.

When developing treatment plans for this population, it is imperative that you keep in close contact with the referring doctor and/or facility. These behaviors can be life-threatening and need to be closely monitored.

Borderline Personality Disorders (BPD) [F60.3]

Though people with BPD are not all at war with their bodies, many do take out their emotional struggles by seriously hurting themselves. Suicide ideation and attempts are not uncommon with more severe BPD clients given their emotional lability, impulse control issues, and self-loathing.

BPD is a complex and often confusing disorder. A full description of etiology, treatment options, prognosis and symptomatology is beyond the scope of this book. However, people with BPD can definitely benefit from equine psychotherapy. Both interpersonal and behavioral issues are effectively addressed by working and bonding with horses. It is best to create treatment goals based on specific behaviors that need to be addressed rather than on the overall Borderline Disorder.

Borderlines often have had a stormy childhood history characterized by trauma, abandonment, and undependable attachment experiences. Unfortunately, this disorder can be generational in that borderline mothers, who have difficulty with impulse control, affect regulation, and an inability to maintain consistent and dependable connections, set the stage for raising children with similar issues. It is hard for a developing child to create a stable sense of self, to develop an inner soothing voice, and to learn to trust others when their homes are characterized by the high drama and chronic crisis typical of borderline mothers. These pervasive developmental injuries leave psychic scars including:

- An inability to self sooth, rendering them highly dependent on external factors (such as people, drugs, cutting) to lower or distract them from intolerable levels of discomfort. The soothing, quiet voice of a mother whispering, "Everything is going to be OK." is sadly missing.

- An overreaction to any behavior that might be construed as potential abandonment ranging from tearful pleading to suicidal attempts.
- A tendency to be easily overwhelmed by uncomfortable emotions leading to avoidance or distancing behavior. Dissociation and psychic numbing or manic, anxiety-driven behavior are common responses.
- Self-abusive behaviors, such as cutting, head banging, etc. can result from a desire to self-punish, or in the case of psychic numbing, to "feel something."
- A penchant to seeing the world, and all those who inhabit it, as either all good or all bad, resulting in tumultuous and unstable relationships. One minute you can be their best friend, the next they are spitting angry fire at you.

Someone with a borderline personality should be in individual therapy *before* adding in equine psychotherapy. Keeping close tabs with the referring therapist and/or agency is imperative.

Slow and steady should be the pace with these fragile people. Bonding with the horse, week after week, might be all that is needed, or tolerated. When working with this population, the calmer, the more forgiving, and the more patient the therapy horse is, the better. Trust will develop slowly, in fits and starts. This is a long and arduous healing journey.

The "go-to" treatment for Borderlines is Dialectical Behavioral Therapy, (DBT) developed by Dr. Marsha Linehan. DBT offers a powerful combination of Cognitive Behavioral Therapy (CBT) and supportive therapy. It easily translates into equine experiential therapy.

In sum, Chapter Eight reviews specific treatment populations found to be particularly amenable to equine experiential psychotherapy. As you can see, many of the emotional and behavioral issues overlap from one group to another which allows for flexibility in treatment planning. It's up to you to be creative and wise!

Chapter Nine

Technical Details in Treatment Planning

Chapter nine reviews some of the basic ethical and reporting requirements needed in running any equine therapy program. Prototypical forms are offered as guidelines in developing ongoing documentation and formalizing communication between referral sources and the program.

The first step is having a client referred to your program. Often the referral comes directly from an independent practitioner or a therapist assigned to the client in an outpatient (clinic) or inpatient setting. You will need a signed HIPPA form which is an official document delineating the parameters of confidentiality. The HIPPA form[18] allows the referring therapist to discuss the case with you.

Request that the referring therapist fill out the following questionnaire which can be used for initial treatment planning and goal setting. It can also be applied as a tool to review progress to date and remaining goals. In addition, it is an excellent instrument to communicate to the referral therapist/clinic any escalation of symptoms or problems which have arisen during treatment.

Therapists' Checklist: Diagnostic Symptomatology

Please specify which issues you are presently addressing with your client. If possible, give examples. Though you will be consulting with the equine therapy team (equine

---

[18]   HIPPA requirements are discussed in Appendix II.

and mental health specialists), any information you can initially provide will be of use to them in creating an initial treatment plan.

What are your goals for equine assisted therapy? Examples might be: helping a detached or angry client develop a trusting relationship with the horse, having a victim of domestic abuse learn assertiveness skills and boundary maintenance skills, or giving a child a chance to safely bond with a receptive friend.

Feel free to include suggestions, including what you have found to be most efficacious and most problematic in your work with this individual.

In addition, if there are other external influences influencing the client, e.g. issues with law enforcement, possibility of abuse, problematic family members, please include this information.

Following is a list of diagnostic categories with behavioral descriptors. Feel free to simply indicate which issues you would like addressed with your client.

PTSD/TRAUMA

1. Dissociation (Please specify: sense of being "spacey", psychic numbing, distraction, depersonalization, etc.)
2. Trust issues: isolation, paranoia
3. Heightened Startle Response/ hyper arousal
4. Flashbacks, issues staying grounded
5. Persistent sense of "survivor's guilt," and unresolved grief
6. Pervasive sense of shame and misplaced sense of responsibility
7. Problems with anger and frustration tolerance
8. Isolation and social withdrawal
9. Possible abuse of alcohol and/or drugs

Comments:

ANXIETY

1. Hyper arousal, restlessness, "keyed up"
2. Issues staying grounded in the here and now
3. Difficulty concentrating and attending to incoming information
4. Chronic worry/obsessing, rumination, dwelling on negative outcomes
5. Physical Manifestations: muscle tension, headaches, stomach issues, sleep disturbances
6. Lack of self-mastery and trust in self and the universe
7. Feeling overwhelmed and paralyzed

Comments:

DEPRESSION

1. Isolation/disconnection
2. Lack of energy, motivation, pleasure
3. Lack of self-mastery, poor ability to make decisions
4. Overdeveloped sense of guilt
5. Sense of *hopelessness* about the future and *helpless* to impact future.
6. Suicidal ideation and/or attempts

Comments:

BORDERLINE/ATTACHMENT DISORDERS

1. Fears of abandonment leading to clinging/demanding behavior
2. Poor affect regulation: anger, irritability, anxiety, flooding
3. Poor sense of personal boundaries
4. Feelings of emptiness and panic

Comments:

SPOUSAL ABUSE

1. Sense of pervasive shame and unworthiness
2. Inability to maintain appropriate boundaries both verbally and physically
3. Isolation/fear
4. Lack of self-efficacy and mastery
5. Misplaced loyalty
6. Enabling
7. Deep sense of guilt and misplaced responsibility

Comments:

ASBERGER SYNDROME

1. Inability to pick up social cues leading to poor boundaries and social isolation and what appears to be a lack of empathy
2. Heightened anxiety around change of routine
3. Overly verbose
4. Eye contact avoidance or tendency to stare
5. Heightened sensitivity to incoming stimuli (please delineate specific sensory issues)

Comments:

DRUG/ALCOHOL ABUSE (must be at least three months sober and committed to some form of treatment, e.g. AA, NA)

1. Particular issues that client is addressing in his/her sobriety, e.g. anger, mistrust, misplacement of responsibility, inappropriate strategies to deal with stress
2. Social stressors resulting from addiction: loss of job, failure of relationship, legal issues, spousal abuse
3. Duel-diagnosis of client
4. ACOA and co-dependency issues

5. Family issues resulting from addiction

Comments:

<u>ADOLSCENT ISSUES:</u> Please give a brief description of client including family dynamics, school issues, and any other information that would be relevant to creating a comprehensive treatment plan.

1. Eating Disorders: please delineate the exact nature of the disorder
2. Oppositional Conduct, e.g. lying, stealing, truancy, court issues, sexual acting out
3. Self-injurious behaviors e.g. cutting, eating disorders, etc.
4. Depression, moodiness, anxiety
5. Aggression
6. Drug/alcohol abuse
7. Isolation separate from depression
8. Sexual acting out
9. Issues with school, e.g. attendance, grades, rule compliance
10. Socialization problems with peers, family members, etc.

Comments:

<u>AD/HD</u>

1. Problems with attention and concentration
2. Inability to sit quietly for extended periods of time appropriate to age level
3. Heightened level of distraction to outside stimuli
4. Disruptive behavior in class, etc.
5. Impulsive responsiveness
6. Interrupts or intrudes on others; poor boundary tolerance
7. Problems with organization and prioritization
8. Acting out at home and in school
9. Inability to attend to details and instructions

Comments:

OTHER DIAGNOSTIC CATEGORIES:

Please include any further information you believe would be helpful in developing a treatment plan for your client.

Now that you are meeting with the client for the first time, it is necessary to do a formal intake and have them (or whoever is responsible) sign all pertinent forms and waivers. The following is a prototype intake form. Please feel free to use it and make any changes necessary to reflect your facility's procedures or requirements.

Equine Assisted Therapy Intake Procedures

Name of Client:

Name of Parent/Guardian:

Address:

Telephone number(s):

Cell phone/contact information:

SS#:

Birthday:

Insurance Information:

Referring Physician/Clinician(s)/School Representative:

1. Name:
   Contact Information:

2. Name:
   Contact Information

3. Name:

   Contact Information

Medical Condition(s): (e.g. allergies, seizure disorders, AD/HD, TBI)

Medication(s):

Diagnosis:

History/Presenting Problem(s):

Behavioral Issues/Goals* (you can ask the client directly what his or her goals might be):

Referral Source: Name_____ Organization_____

Contact information: _____ Email: _____

Mailing Information: _____

Intake Clinician:

Date of Intake:

Forms:

   "Hold Harmless" form: _____
   Emergency Consent Form to Obtain Medical Treatment: _____
   HIPPA release forms: _____
   Medical forms: _____

Comments:

Setting up initial equine assisted therapy treatment plan

TREATMENT PLAN PROTOTYPE FOR PSYCHOTHERAPISTS AND EQUINE SPECIALISTS (ES)

After an original assessment of the client and communication with treating clinicians, the psychotherapist is responsible for generating a preliminary treatment plan including short and long-term goals. The initial report/assessment needs to contain all relevant medical conditions, medications, and emergency numbers including the referring clinician's contact information. If a formal diagnosis was offered, that should also be noted. HIPPA forms need to be signed by the client or in the case of a minor, the responsible adult.[19] This legally enables the psychotherapist and Equine Specialist to discuss the case with each other and referring clinicians. All of the above will become part of the client's ongoing file.

The original treatment plan is discussed and refined with the Equine Specialist (ES). The ES is responsible for choosing appropriate equine/human activities geared to the client's issues. Selecting an appropriate horse might be discussed at this point.

Preliminary Client Meeting

A preliminary session should be held with the client (in case of a minor), the client's guardian, the psychotherapist, and the equine specialist to:

- Discuss and refine the initial treatment plan including reviewing treatment goals with the client and team.
- Review the stable's rules and regulations, e.g. no cell phones or iPads! (There could be a safe place in the Barn to store electronic equipment.)
- Educate the client about the basic "do's" and "don'ts" around horses including appropriate attire in the barn.
- Introduce the client to his or her therapy horse.

---

[19] This second HIPPA form allows the equine team to discuss the case with each other and the referring therapist or responsible adult.

- Tour the barn and review where the client is to wait for his or her therapist and where basic equipment is stored (e.g. grooming kits, lead lines, etc.).
- Sign all necessary release and liability forms.
- Answer any questions the client and/or custodian have.
- Have the client pick out a grooming kit which will be theirs for the duration of their equine therapy experience.
- You might also consider having the client sign an "equine therapy" contract which might include such things as: agreeing to treat the horse with respect and dignity, maintaining a quiet demeanor in the barn and around the horses, being responsible for returning all equipment used during the session to its appropriate place, etc. This could be used to help elucidate some of the rules and behaviors that need to be maintained to ensure the safety of the horses and humans.

This first group meeting is also a way of acquainting everyone with the team approach employed in equine therapy. If appropriate, the horse could be at liberty near the meeting so he or she can be incorporated in the team from the beginning.

The client will be encouraged to be an active participant in creating and establishing their own goals and objectives. Empowerment, decision making, and interpersonal dynamics are all touched upon during this first group meeting. When dealing with a child, the above needs to be simplified to allow the child to feel part of the process.

Treatment Plan meetings should be scheduled bimonthly or monthly, as deemed appropriate for the particular case.

Case Files

Each client should have a dedicated case file which needs to contain the following information and documents:

Name

Address

Social Security Number

Birthdate

Client Contact Information

Relation to Client

Telephone (cell, home)

Email

Address

Professional Contact Information, e.g. referring therapist, clinic, school, physician

Telephone

Email

Address

Contact Person (in case of a clinic, school, hospital, etc.)

Presenting Diagnosis:

Preexisting Medical Conditions:

Medications:

Each Client File should also contain all release forms (HIPPA, Liability ("hold-harmless" agreement), an emergency consent form to obtain medical treatment, etc.).

In addition, after each session, progress notes should be included as part of the case file. In particular, therapeutic activities, observations, and objectives for further sessions should be documented. This ongoing treatment narrative ensures a continuation of goals from one session to the next and from one therapeutic team to another. Many funding agencies require a quarterly or annual progress report and these notes can be very useful!

Liability

Every facility that offers EEP must have equine liability insurance. All members of the treatment team need to carry personal malpractice and liability insurance. Supposedly, licensed psychotherapists' malpractice will cover them when doing equine psychotherapy. To date, I've never had to validate this, thank the heavens!

You can find liability carriers via the internet or by referral from others in the field.

In sum, setting up your treatment program with the necessary legal, ethical, and reporting requirement is imperative to run a complex organization offering equine psychotherapy. And, believe me, organizing horses, treating therapists, volunteers, anxious parents and scared clients, and perhaps a barn cat or three, is complex! Add in the business part, e.g. paying bills, writing reports, organizing vet and furrier visits, making sure everyone is fed and brushed, and ensuring that the tack room doesn't look like a typhoon blew through it, makes each day a tactical challenge! The more organized and efficient you can be, the more time you have to muck the stalls...and isn't that what it's all about!

PART III

Beyond Words: A Photo Essay

Getting to Know You.

Look at me! I'm a wonderful thing!

This is my friend.

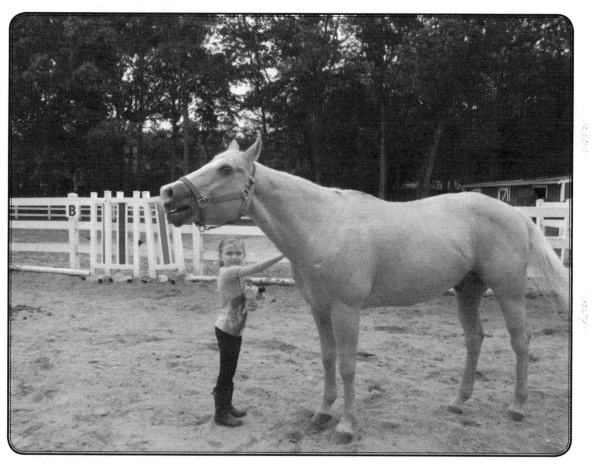

And he's so happy to see me!

I'm beginning to trust you.

Opening my heart to you. I am no longer afraid.

It's so nice being with you too! I'm so comfortable with you.

We're all in this together…and it's fun!

Sometimes a hard journey is better with friends.

And sometimes it's fun even if there are obstacles along the way!

Along my journey, fragile parts of me might get wounded.

How do we make sense of the events in our lives? Our personal history?

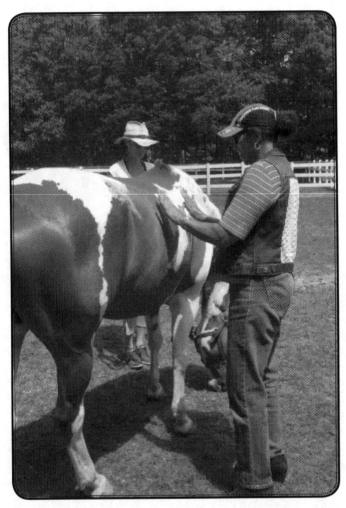

I am humbled that you allow me to come close,
to share your energy with me.

I can put the full weight of my needs on you, you'll support me.

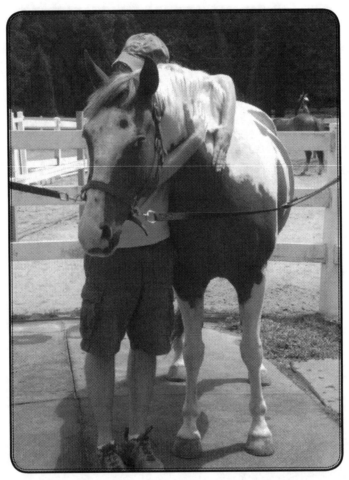

I feel your compassion and caring. I can rest awhile with you.

All I ever needed was a hug….and reassurance
that everything is going to be ok.

It's been a wonderful journey. I wonder what tomorrow will bring?

Epilouge: On Behalf of Equine Specialists

All of us who have been drawn to equine experiential therapy are healers whether we come from the equine or psychological worlds. No matter what path brings us to equine psychotherapy, the motivation and calling are the same; to help people lead more meaningful and emotionally enriching lives via their connections with horses.

I have been riding horses most of my life. I grew up in Pony Camp and competed in combined training throughout high school. After college, I became a professional trainer specializing in starting young horses and working with those that were considered difficult and dangerous. Always drawn to the healing arts, I became a PATH Certified Therapeutic Riding Instructor in 2004. In 2009, I added Equine Specialist in Mental Health and expanded my interests to include not just what horses could provide for people with disabilities, but how horses could facilitate mental health and emotional healing.

I first met Alita via the EFMHE list server. Her interest in developing workshops for people with emotional issues dovetailed with my growing interest in this aspect of equine therapy. From ongoing dialogues, Alita and I were able to integrate the most important elements of our practices. We both agreed that while there are many approaches to equine facilitated therapy, the most powerful interventions focus on developing the relationship between client and horse. In relationship, we learn about ourselves and are offered opportunities to change and grow. The horse, as any good psychotherapist does, provides a relationship free of judgement, expectation, or criticism. They simply accept what enters their world and respond to it accordingly sensing the energy and intention behind the physical body.

We may not be able to change our past experiences, but we *can* adapt our energy and thus transform ourselves and our emotional response to external circumstances. Horses are masters at teaching us this skill. It is my experience that incorporating breathing techniques, mindfulness, grounding, and heightened awareness are essential elements for restoring a horse to a calm, relaxed state when he becomes agitated. Alita also includes these practices in her work, particularly when helping people recover from traumatic experiences that seem to be trapped in the body. We both have had plenty of experience with a phenomenon known as "amygdala hijacking," when a person (or horse) shows an extreme overreaction to a non-threatening stimulus. I had learned to gently release these triggers through gentle bodywork and thereby restore the horse's nervous system to a parasympathetic state (also referred to in horse lingo as going back to grazing). This somatic approach to healing the mind was completely congruent to Alita's approach to healing trauma in humans. My fascination with the subject bloomed, and Alita kindly helped to educate me in the latest theories of psychotherapy.

During that time I was dealing with my own personal trauma that had resurfaced in my life. Horrendous enough on its own, the matter became a subject of media attention that forced me to face a terrifying shadow in a very public way. It's funny how things come into your life at just the right time, and I am convinced that Alita showed up when I needed her most. Her positive energy and constant encouragement helped pull me through a very dark time. I might have crawled into a hole and hidden myself from the world, but realizing that I would not be judged, that my gifts were still valid despite the darkness that threatened to envelop me, helped me to endure. That someone I respected and trusted understood the significance of what I had discovered, was just what I needed to be able to move out of that awful place and go forward in my life with a measure of confidence. I was grateful for the opportunity to share with her all I knew about the nature of horses, and in return I was able to grow in my own abilities and knowledge of what it means to heal from an emotional wound. Healing is not a quick fix, there are no short cuts or instant remedies, it is a process that we must learn to embody in our lives from moment to moment, in real life situations that may seem overwhelming and threaten to topple our emotional balance. Solid relationships are crucial to staying afloat on the sometimes turbulent sea of life. Alita saw something in me that others missed, she saw my heart and she helped it to heal. She helped me find the courage to heal others and help them through their troubles. This is the very nature of what the horses can teach us. We help each other, we are not in this alone, and each one of us is responsible for finding our own joy. When we find it, we can help create a joyful space for others.

I've been fortunate to have learned from some of the greatest pioneers in the field of equine facilitated psychotherapy. There are many approaches out there, and I don't believe that one size fits all. What I love about Alita's approach to incorporating horses into the therapeutic process, is she puts the relationship first, she honors the horse as a sentient being, and she embodies all of the great qualities of horsiness in her approach to working with people and horses. Her sense of humor and playfulness are essential to good horsemanship. She also understands when it's time to be serious, when we must incorporate mindfulness and clear boundary setting into the interaction.

Equine therapy differs from other forms of therapy in that it includes a very large animal with a mind of its own. Recognizing the sentient nature of the horse and giving him leeway to guide a session and offer feedback includes risk, including a knowledgeable and experienced horse person in the equation is crucial. The equine specialist differs from an instructor in that she must step back and allow the client to interact without interference, often refraining from teaching and simply maintaining a safe space for the client to learn through direct experience. While this technique can offer insight that other interventions cannot, it also has the potential to be stressful or confusing for the horse. Horses will usually communicate their feelings through benign body language, but if unheeded these warnings could escalate into kicking out, biting, or other unwanted behaviors. The equine specialist must know her horses well and intervene if any situation becomes unsafe. The equine specialist should have a close relationship with the horse, so that she can provide him with the consistency and support he needs to feel safe and understand what is being asked of him. The relationship between the horse and the equine specialist should be well established before bringing clients into the picture. In a similar vein, the mental health professional maintains the physical and emotional safety of the client.

Whether offering feedback that we can use to make important changes in how we engage in relationship, showing us how to release tension and anxiety and restore calm to the nervous system, guiding us to be more effective leaders and teammates, or simply absorbing our emotional chaos and helping us let go of those things that are no longer serving us, horses have time and again proven to be willing, generous benefactors. I believe that this is due to the long standing relationship between horses and humans. As far as they are concerned, we are part of their herd, and our well-being is closely linked to their own. Their very survival depends on whether humanity acts with compassion for other living things. How we treat animals, the earth, and our fellow humans determines the future of our shared planet. Horses are experts at getting back to grazing, hanging peacefully with their herd, and growing strong and loving bonds. They remind us that peace and balance are the ultimate goal. In this simplicity, we can be whole again.

Horsemanship is a constant balancing act embodying a gentle strength that can be hard to master. The horses silently teach us this character trait that is so important as we navigate life. They remind us to get real. They bring us into the present. They respond to who we are in the moment. Alita understands this and has described a simple, straight forward approach for incorporating horses into therapeutic sessions in a way that honors the best of what horses can provide.

The synergy that gets created when we therapists; the equine specialist, the psychotherapist and, of course, the horse, pool our talents becomes a remarkable force for emotional change and healing. We work to remain open to each other's gifts, what we can learn from each other, and teach each other. With all that love and hopefulness, care and attention wonderful things can happen....and often do.

Stacey Carter, Founder and Director of *Heart Centered Horsemanship*
PATH Int'l Certified Instructor
Equine Specialist in Mental Health and Learning

Appendix I

Certification and Credentialing Organizations

My goal, in this section, is simply to present to the reader some of the licensing and credentialing options that now exist in the EEP field. I am not advocating for any of them; it is up to you to find the one that best fits your needs, goals, and personality.

All of the equine organizations emphasize the ethical treatment of horses as well as specific training requirements for all involved disciplines.

For further information, you can contact any of the organizations directly or read their websites.

NARHA - The North American Riding for the Handicapped Association & EFMHA - Equine Facilitated Mental Health Association

The formalized practice of therapeutic riding emerged in Europe in the early 1950's as a technique for working with people with disabilities. The North American Riding for the Handicapped Association (NARHA) was founded in 1969 introducing therapeutic riding for the disabled to the US and Canada.

The use of horses to improve the quality of life for people with disabilities was extended to clients with psychological difficulties as horses proved to be wonderful co-therapists in dealing with emotional issues. Equine Facilitated Mental Health Association (EFMHA), which started in 1996 as a division of NARHA, was created to establish standards and practices in this field.

The vision of the group is to promote professional credibility and to achieve public confidence in the transformative value of equine-human interaction.

CBEIP - The Certification Board of Equine Interaction Professionals (www. cbeip.org)

Barbara Rector,[20] founder and director of Adventures in Awareness (A1A) writes that, "The Certification Board of Equine Interaction Professionals, in my world view, is the gold standard of excellence for practitioners serious about Equine Interactions with a Sentient Being who also contributes to the healing process."[21]

CBEIP does not offer a particular training or credential. It acts more as a licensing board for the EEP community requiring applicants to have attained a certain level of training and to sit for an exam. Details of the requirements can be found at their website. CBEIP is a credentialing organization. Certification is just one part of the credentialing process.

Barbara continues, "…None of these organizations (PATH, EPONA, EAGALA) which train and teach offer legal true certifications in the sense of passing the bar exam or the medical boards. They all offer "Certificates of Completion" of the particular curriculum being taught. Many in our world mistakenly refer to these completion certificates as "certification" including the organizations themselves."

EAGALA – Equine Growth and Learning Association (www.eagala.org)

EAGALA is one of the more behaviorally based programs. The relationship with the horse is *not* the central tenet of this approach. Specific exercises are offered and how the clients approach and resolve the exercises are discussed. This program uses ground work.

---

[20]   Barbara Rector served two terms on the Board of Trustees for NARHA – now Professional Association of Therapeutic Horsemanship International (PATH Intl). and nine years on the Medical Committee developing and reviewing Standards, Safety Guidelines and Therapeutic Riding facility protocols. She is considered on one of the master therapists in the field of equine experiential psychotherapy. Barbara's book, *Adventures in Awareness: Learning With the Help of Horses* is available through Amazon as paperback or eBook.

[21]   Private Correspondence, (10/20/16)

EAGALA has certification programs for both mental health professionals (MH) and for equine specialists (EQ). It requires that all mental health specialists (MHs) must have appropriate licensure from their state.

EPONA (www.taoofequus.com)

The EPONA model *emphases* the relationship between the client and the horse. It offers an eclectic approach incorporating differing therapeutic and spiritual leanings. Psychotherapists must also be licensed in the state and country in which they practice. EPONA was developed by Linda Kohanov, who has written a number of excellent books on the topic of equine psychotherapy. This program uses ground work.

PATH - The Professional Association of Therapeutic Horsemanship (pathintl@path.org)

PATH INTERNATIONAL deals with both mental health issues and physical disabilities and concentrates on mounted work.

In this model, to become certified, a Mental Health Specialist "…must be knowledgeable in horsemanship and understands how to work with a mental health therapist and/or educator to best meet the client's needs and keep the lesson safe. ESMHLs also have a general knowledge of mental health and education processes."

"A licensed mental health professional must work with a PATH Intl. certified equine specialist in mental health during all EFT sessions. The Mental Health Professional current professional liability insurance and has additional training, education, and supervision in EFP." (PATH Intl. 2011b)

In "Strides" the PATH International magazine, Vol. 22, no. 1 (winter, 2016) there is a section devoted to "Certification Demystified" which deals with the Equine Specialist. For further clarification, please refer to the PATH Intl. web page.

Adventures In Awareness (AIA) (www.adventuresinawareness.net)

I admit to a biased review of AIA since I found it a wonderful educational, practical and hands-on training experience. AIA is a training program, not a certification or credentialing organization.

AIA offers training in both ground and mounted work. The emphasis is on the healing potential of horse/human interactions by incorporating structured exercises to deepen those connections. AIA is a very ethical, horse-appreciative approach.

The three day intensive, one on one, training program is an ideal way of immersing yourself in the EEP world. You get the rare opportunity to learn from one of the master therapists in the field. Both the psychotherapists and horse specialists I've met agreed that this is a powerful and enlightening experience. AIA also offers various training seminars as well as an internship program.

Most of the certification programs have specific training requirements including but not limited to: years of practice in the field of expertise (equine specialists, mental health practitioners), licensure in their respective states (mental health practitioners), completion of training as defined by each association, and continued education hours to maintain certification status.

You can get certified in either specialty or both if you are qualified. Each one has a strict code of ethics which protects both the clients *and* the horses.

There are a myriad of programs to choose from and the choices seem to be growing exponentially! Credentialing can be an expensive, time-consuming endeavor so it makes sense to take your time, read the descriptions, and talk to people in the field before you make a decision. My belief, already stated, is that as much training and approaches as you can experience, the better for you, your horse, and your client. And, it's fun!

Appendix II

HIPAA Privacy Rule and Sharing Information Related to Mental Health
U.S. Department of Health and Human Services

<u>Background</u>

The Health Insurance Portability and Accountability Act (HIPAA) Privacy Rule provides consumers with important privacy rights and protections with respect to their health information, including important controls over how their health information is used and disclosed by health plans and health care providers. Ensuring strong privacy protections is critical to maintaining individuals' trust in their health care providers and willingness to obtain needed health care services, and these protections are especially important where very sensitive information is concerned, such as mental health information. At the same time, the Privacy Rule recognizes circumstances arise where health information may need to be shared to ensure the patient receives the best treatment and for other important purposes, such as for the health and safety of the patient or others. The Rule is carefully balanced to allow uses and disclosures of information—including mental health information— for treatment and these other purposes with appropriate protections.

In this guidance, we address some of the more frequently asked questions about when it is appropriate under the Privacy Rule for a health care provider to share the protected health information of a patient who is being treated for a mental health condition. We clarify when HIPAA permits health care providers to:

o   Communicate with a patient's family members, friends, or others involved in the patient's care;

o   Communicate with family members when the patient is an adult;

o   Communicate with the parent of a patient who is a minor; o Consider the patient's capacity to agree or object to the sharing of their information;

o   Involve a patient's family members, friends, or others in dealing with patient failures to adhere to medication or other therapy;

o   Listen to family members about their loved ones receiving mental health treatment;

o   Communicate with family members, law enforcement, or others when the patient presents a serious and imminent threat of harm to self or others; and

o   Communicate to law enforcement about the release of a patient brought in for an emergency psychiatric hold.

In addition, the guidance provides relevant reminders about related issues, such as the heightened protections afforded to psychotherapy notes by the Privacy Rule, a parent's right to access the protected health information of a minor child as the child's personal representative, the potential applicability of Federal alcohol and drug abuse confidentiality regulations or state laws that may provide more stringent protections for the information than HIPAA, and the intersection of HIPAA and FERPA in a school setting.

Bibliography

Ainspan, Nathan D. and Penk, Walter (eds.) *Returning War' Wounded, Injured, and Ill.* Westport, CT: Security International, 2008.

Bancroft, Lundy. *Why Does He Do That? Inside the Minds of Angry and Controlling Men.* New York: Berkley Books, 2002.

Beck, Aaron. *Cognitive Therapy and Emotional Disorders.* New York: Penguin Books, 1976.

Burka, Jane B., Ph.D. & Yuen, Lenora M. Ph.D. *Procrastination- Why You Do It. What to Do About It NOW.* Cambridge, Mass.: Da Cappo Press, 2008.

Burns, David. *Feeling Good: The New Mood Therapy.* New York: Harper Collins, 2008.

Dorotik, Claire, M.A. *On the back of a horse: Harnessing the healing power of the human-equine bond.* Bloomington, Indiana: IUniverse, 2011.

Gilbert, Paul, & Choden. *Mindful Compassion.* Oakland: New Harbinger Publications, 2013.

Goleman, Daniel. *Emotional Intelligence.* New York: Bantam Books, 1995.

Greenspan, Miriam. *Healing Through the Dark Emotions: The Wisdom of Grief, Fear and Despair.* Boston, Mass.: Shambhala Publications, 2003.

Hamilton, Allan J., *M.D. Zen Mind Zen Horse* North Adams, MA: Story Publishing, 2011.

Hayes, Tim. *Riding Home: The Power of Horses to Heal.* New York: St. Martin's Press, 2015.

Jung, C.G. *Analytical Psychology in Theory and Practice.* New York: A Vintage Book, 1970.

    The Practice of Psychotherapy: Essays on the Psychology of the Transference and Other Subjects. Volume 16 of the Collected Works. New York: Princeton University Press, 1966.

Kohanov, Linda. *The Tao of Equus.* California: New World Press, 2001.

    The Power of the Herd, A Nonpredatory Approach to Social Intelligence, Leadership, and Innovation. California: New World Press, 2013.

Kornfield, Jack. *The Wise Heart, A Guide to the Universal Teachings of Buddhist Psychology.* New York: Bantam Books, 2009.

    The Art of Forgiveness, Lovingkindness, and Peace, New York: Bantam Books, 2008.

    A Path With Heart: A Guide Through the Perils and Promises of Spiritual Life. New York: Bantam Books, 1993.

Lamott, Anne. *Bird by Bird: Some Instructions on Writing and Life.* New York: Anchor Books, 1995.

    Traveling Mercies: Some Thoughts on Faith. New York, Anchor Books, 2000.

Lauson, Christine Ann. *Understanding The Borderline Mother: Helping Her Children Transcend the Intense, Unpredictable, and Volatile Relationship.* Lanmham: Rowan & Littlefield Publishers, Inc. 2004.

Lavender, Don. *Equine-Utilised Psychotherapy.* London: Mrunalini Press Limited, 2006.

Levine, Peter. *Waking the Tiger: Healing Trauma.* Berkeley, California: North Atlantic Books, 1997.

McCormick, Adele von Rust Ph.D & McCormick, Marlena Deborah. *Horse Sense and the Human Heart:* Deerfield, Florida: Health Communications, Inc.1997.

Miller, Alice. *The Drama of the Gifted Child, The Search For the True Self.* New York: Basic Books, 1997.

Morris, David J. *The Evil Hours: A Biography of Post-Traumatic Stress Disorder.* New York: Eamon Dolan Book, 2015.

Rao, Vani & Vaishnavi, Sandeep. *The Traumatized Brain: A Family Guide to Understanding Mood, Memory & Behavior After Brain Injury.* Baltimore, MA. Johns Hopkins University Press, 2015.

Rector, Barbara. *Adventures in Awareness.* New York: AuthorHouse, 2015.

Real, Terrence. *I Don't Want To Talk About It: Overcoming the Secret Legacy of Male Depression.* New York: Scribner, 1998.

Shambo, Leigh, MSW. *The Listening Heart.* Chehalis, WA: Human-Equine Alliances For Learning, 2013.

Shay, Johnathan, Ph.D. *Odysseus In America: Combat Trauma and the Trials of Homecoming.* New York: Scribner, 2002.

Siegel, Daniel. *Mindsight: The New Science of Personal Transformation.* New York: Bantam Books, 2011.

Swift, Saly. *Centered Riding.* Vermont: Trafalgar Square, 1985.

Alita H. Buzel

Alita H. Buzel

Thich, Hanh Nhat. The Miracle of Mindfulness: An introduction to the Practice of Meditation. Beacon Press, 1999.

Kay Trotter. *Harnessing the Power of Equine Assisted Counseling*: New York: Routeledge, 2012.

Van Der Kolk, Bessel, M.D. *The Body Keeps The Score: Brain, Mind, and Body in the Healing of Trauma*. New York: Viking, 2014.

Walters, Lisa. *In The Field With Horses*: California: Over and Above Press, 2014.

Acknowledgements

I would like to acknowledge all the pioneer souls who have cleared a path so that we, who are just now entering the study of equine psychotherapy, could follow in their footsteps. In particular, I would like to thank Barbara Rector for her wisdom and guidance and Stacey Carter for her encouragement and gentle teachings. A note of gratitude goes to my editor, Deborah Odell and to Allison Wade for her photographic genius. I send a hug to Rebecca Wilson who offered her horses, stable, and insights to my endeavors. And, finally, to Marta Elders, who taught me to courageously throw my heart over the hurdle and trust that the rest will follow.

Index

Printed in the United States
By Bookmasters